D0464569

The Novels of Colin Wilson

THE NOVELS OF COLIN WILSON

by
Nicolas Tredell

VISION
and
BARNES & NOBLE

Vision Press Limited
11–14 Stanhope Mews West
London SW7 5RD

and

Barnes & Noble Books
81 Adams Drive
Totowa, NJ 07512

ISBN (UK) 0 85478 035 1
ISBN (US) 0 389 20280 0

Printed and bound in Great Britain by
Unwin Brothers Ltd.,
Old Woking, Surrey.
Phototypeset by Galleon Photosetting,
Ipswich, Suffolk.
MCMLXXXII

Contents

Acknowledgements

Grateful acknowledgements for quotations to: Colin Wilson; his agents, Bolt and Watson Ltd.; Victor Gollancz Ltd. (*Ritual in the Dark, Adrift in Soho, The World of Violence, The Outsider, The Strength to Dream*); Hodder and Stoughton Ltd. (*The Occult*); Hutchinson Ltd. (*Bernard Shaw, Introduction to the New Existentialism, Poetry and Mysticism*); Weidenfeld and Nicolson Ltd. (*The Mind Parasites*); Cecil Woolf Ltd. (*Voyage to a Beginning*); The Bodley Head Ltd. (*Contraries* by Stuart Holroyd); Faber and Faber Ltd. (*The Ordinary Universe* by Dennis Donoghue); The Society of Authors on behalf of the Bernard Shaw Estate; Peter Owen Ltd. (*The Angry Decade* by Kenneth Allsop); William Heinemann Ltd. (*English Journey* by J. B. Priestley); University of Notre Dame Press (*Structural Fabulation* by Robert Scholes).

1

A Writer's Development

Colin Wilson has told his own life story up to the age of thirty-five in *Voyage to a Beginning* (1968), and some of his other books contain autobiographical sketches. Sidney Campion's *The World of Colin Wilson* (1962) provides a lot of information about Wilson's childhood and early manhood. In time, a full biography will no doubt be written, and this should be fascinating, not only because Wilson is a remarkable man, but because of the light it could shed on the complex cultural history of our time. Here, I shall briefly outline the main events of his life, with special emphasis upon the cultural influences on his development—the influences that have helped to shape him into a writer.

Colin Wilson was born in 1931, into a working-class family in the East Midlands town of Leicester. Though Leicester is a prosperous town, and its history dates back to Roman times, it can seem curiously featureless. Visiting it on his 'English Journey' in 1934, J. B. Priestley commented:

> The town seems to have no atmosphere of its own . . . it is hard to believe that anything much has ever happened there.[1]

Leicester's chief industries are hosiery, and boots and shoes. Wilson's father was a boot-and-shoe operative, who earned £3.10s. (old currency) a week throughout the 1930s.[2] Money was tight, and cultural stimulation small.[3] It was an apparently unpropitious environment for a writer.

There were two sides to Wilson's childhood. He was a first child and a first grandchild; as a result, he was spoiled, especially

7

by his grandparents. He has called this 'the most essential fact about my childhood'.[4] He was also frequently told that he was 'born lucky'. As Richard Hoggart has pointed out, the belief in 'luck' was strong among the urban working class earlier this century. Luck was something you were born with or you were not, but if you were, it would help you enormously in life.[5] All this created in Wilson a sense of confidence and optimism which has never left him, and which fuels the affirmative drive of his work, although he now believes that 'luck' can be controlled through will-power and self-discipline.

Wilson felt himself to be further privileged in that, when he was 4, his parents moved out of a small flat into a council house. This had a back and front garden, and stood in an area of wide-tree-lined roads. It contrasted favourably with the small terraced houses, in narrow streets near the town centre, where most of his relatives lived. He recalls:

> In all my childhood, I never went into a house that made me wish *we* lived in it. . . . So I remained free of any social ambitions, and remained completely unaware of myself as a member of a 'social class'.[6]

Wilson's avoidance of a conventional career or university education, and his spectacular rise to fame in defiance of class barriers meant, furthermore, that he never became conscious of class as an obstacle in later life. For an English novelist, he has remained remarkably unconcerned with class, or indeed with any aspect of man in society, and he has never been tempted to explain alienation in social and political terms.

Wilson's childhood also had a negative side, however. The tensions created by lack of money often made his mother miserable; she was to have two more boys and a girl, but she made her first child her confidant; Wilson says that this 'manufactured a morbid sensitivity' in him.[7] Sometimes his morbidity reached an extreme: one incident typifies this. One morning, he asked his mother what he could take to school to eat in his mid-morning break. She replied: 'There's no food in the house.' Wilson comments: 'I [was] oppressed all the morning by a horrible sense of tragedy: we were starving.'[8] At lunchtime, however, he learnt that his mother had only meant that she had temporarily run out of food, and had not yet been shopping to buy some more. It is, of course, an incident that would be less likely to occur in a middle-class home.

This experience can be seen as the forerunner, the 'objective correlative', of the metaphysical 'vastations' Wilson was later to undergo: the feeling that the apparently secure human world was an illusion, that life was only 'an escape . . . from some ultimate pain on the other side of existence'.[9] Two worlds: confident optimism and acute pessimism; an intense sense of value and a fundamental nihilism. It is these extremes that Wilson's work, especially his novels, will explore.

By conventional standards of literacy, Wilson's cultural environment as a child was gravely deprived. He says that, throughout his childhood, he 'never met anyone who was in the least interested in ideas, or in knowledge for its own sake'.[10] Until he was 10, he read only a weekly comic. Tales of death and violence were the main stimuli of his imagination, and he became known to the other boys in his neighbourhood as a teller of horror stories. The cinema was a major influence. From the age of 6 or 7, he often went to the cinema, sometimes as much as four times a week. His grandparents gave him free tickets which they received for displaying cinema posters in their window. Wilson comments:

> I owe a very considerable debt to the cinema. . . . Famous musicians and theatre critics have written about the revelation of attending the theatre or opera for the first time; but every working class child has the same experience when he first goes to the cinema.[11]

The cinema also introduced him to classical music, through the soundtrack accompanying some films.

Wilson's early exposure to film would have given him a strong sense of the imaginative stimulus that the popular and sensational can provide. It would also have contributed to his belief that, in a novel, the overall impact may be more important than the detail. We do not 'close read' films (though video technology may now facilitate an analogous process). Individual scenes may be weak, but we do not have time to dwell on them as the film unrolls. The total effect can still be impressive.

From the age of 10, Wilson began to read all the books his mother borrowed from the public library. Public libraries were hereafter to become important cultural resources for him. His mother was especially fond of the work of D. H. Lawrence, but Wilson never shared her affection. Apart from Lawrence, she liked two main kinds of books: sex-and-violence gangster novels, of the type which had started to spread from America in the '30s, and the novels about life in slum districts in England. She also liked *True Detective* and *True Romances* magazines, and Wilson read all these as well. He found that the *True Detective* magazines and the gangster novels conveyed a sense of brutal nihilism, of a 'world without values'.[12] They also, however, contributed to the interest in crime, especially murder, which has remained with Wilson, and has been pursued in both his fiction and non-fiction.

An alternative to the 'world without values' was provided by his discovery of science. This was due to a book called *The Marvels and Mysteries of Science*, which was given to him as a present. Wilson has stressed the importance of this discovery: it opened up an impersonal world of knowledge and significance that provided an escape from the triviality of his environment. He also discovered science fiction: at the age of 11, his grand-father gave him a science fiction magazine. It was the first time he had seen one, and he found it more exciting than anything he had ever read previously. He became a science fiction addict and soon built up a large collection of magazines such as *Amazing Stories, Thrilling Stories* and *Fantasy Magazine*. H. G. Wells became the writer he most admired, though as a story-teller rather than a writer concerned with ideas. There are important links between Wilson and Wells.

Wilson has emphasized that it was not merely the sensational aspects of science fiction which appealed to him. Science fiction, like science itself, seemed to engage with issues of the utmost importance to mankind; in contrast to the gangster novels, it conveyed a profound sense of values. This reaction to science fiction is common in intelligent boys.

It is very important to bear in mind, in considering Wilson's novels, that his chief experience of imaginative literature up to the age of 13 was provided by sensational popular fiction: sex and violence gangster novels, and science fiction and fantasy tales. A major feature of Wilson's novels is their use of elements and forms from popular fiction. Of course, he is not the only modern novelist to use such materials, but he does so more wholeheartedly, and with less attempt to safeguard his 'serious' credentials, than anyone else. We can see, however, that his childhood reading had taught him that such despised modes could be a vital imaginative stimulus. Certainly they may also have adverse effects—a blunting of the sensibilities, the inculcation of a taste for sensation at the expense of subtlety—but, in a culturally deprived situation, that imaginative stimulus may be more important.[13]

Wilson's childhood reading, and his cinema-going, had further taught him that popular modes could symbolize as well as undermine serious concerns. For example, the two extremes in his own life, of nihilism and profound purposiveness, were symbolized by gangster novels and science fiction tales respectively. The popular and serious co-existed and interacted in his own early experience, and a distinction between them has never been rigorously enforced in his work. This is especially true of his novels. His use of popular materials in those novels can be seen as an attempt to harness the imaginative and symbolic energies of such materials, of which he became conscious as a child, to serious ends, and thus to redeem his early reading.

Science fiction also introduced Wilson, in an inevitably garbled way, to the ideas of Einstein, and he read a number of laymen's guides that dealt with relativity, such as Sir James Jeans' *The Mysterious Universe* (1930). Summaries of knowledge and laymen's guides to ideas were to play an increasingly important part in Wilson's development, as they had done in the development of H. G. Wells.[14] A popular textbook of psychology introduced him to the theories of Freud, Jung and Adler, and Adler's theory of the Power-instinct struck him as a 'revelation'.[15] It was the joint influence of Adler and Einstein that compelled him to begin his writing career. He produced a series of 'Subjective Essays' and, in the school summer holiday of 1944, he set out to write a book summarizing all the scientific knowledge of mankind. As his sources, he used books from the public library, and a six-volume encyclopaedia he had bought at a church bazaar called *Practical Knowledge for All*. By the time he returned to school, he had written about 90,000 words, but had seen the impossibility of the project, in view of the vast extent of modern scientific knowledge.

It was the first sign, however, of his desire, since manifested in his published works, to assimilate, synthesize, and communicate a wide range of facts and ideas; to produce, in fact, the kind of books that were so important in his own early self-education. In this respect too, he resembles H. G. Wells. It is also significant that Wilson's first written work was not fiction, although, as we have seen, he had been an oral story-teller. Wilson's energies as a writer have never been directed solely towards fiction; as with Wells, fiction has always taken its place, a unique but not an exclusive one, in a general enquiry into human existence.

The articles on literature in *Practical Knowledge for All* introduced Wilson to the traditional corpus of English literature, and told him of Palgrave's *Golden Treasury of Songs and Poems*. He developed a passion for poetry, and came to know the *Golden Treasury* almost by heart. The writers who impressed him at this time seem to have been Chaucer, Spenser, Ben Jonson, Milton, Coleridge, Lamb, and Macaulay.[16] It is notable that Shakespeare was not among them: Wilson has remained unrepentant about the low opinion of Shakespeare that he shares with Tolstoy and, more significantly in terms of influence, with Shaw. Poetry offered an imaginative universe which contrasted with the nihilistic world of the gangster novels: it approached, from a different direction, the vision of science.

Wilson's early teens were a period of intense reading, writing and thinking. He was acutely isolated: without friends of his own age, without any adults to whom he could talk about his deepest obsessions and desires, without any cultural context responsive to his needs. This meant that he had to begin creating his own context and, given the extreme, metaphysical nature of his concerns, this context could not be a limited one: it had to aim at a complete mapping of reality, at being a culture in the full sense: a structuring of the universe.

At this time, Wilson was dominated by a sense of futility. In T. S. Eliot he found a poet who expressed that futility inimitably. Eliot, living in a fragmented and materialistic culture which could not satisfy his aspirations for wholeness and spiritual fulfilment, had also had to create his own context. Wilson has described Eliot as the second very great influence on his work and thinking.[17] The greatest influence of all, however, was to enter his life through a new cultural medium: B.B.C. Radio's Third Programme, which began on 29 September 1946.[18] This became important in furthering his musical education, but was even more important in that, in its very first week of transmission, he switched on to find himself listening to a play: Bernard Shaw's *Man and Superman.*

Listening to Shaw, Wilson believed that he had, for the first time, found a fellow-spirit: a man who was concerned with all the problems of meaning and purpose in human life that preoccupied him, and who, furthermore, offered an antidote to futility: evolutionary optimism. Wilson read through all his plays and developed an admiration for Shaw that has never left him; he still regards him as the greatest European writer since Dante.[19]

Wilson left the Gateway Secondary Technical School in Leicester in 1947, at the age of 16. Formal education had meant little to him; he has said: 'I learned a disproportionately small amount from my eleven years' schooling.'[20] For the next eight years, until the publication of *The Outsider*, his life was to take on the aspects of a *Künstlerroman* and a picaresque novel. He would travel through the 'lower depths' of post-war Britain: jobs in offices and factories, on building sites and in cafés, often tedious, hard and low-paid; National Service; months on the dole; seedy lodgings; sleeping rough. By external standards, he would become a drifter, a forerunner of the dropouts and hippies of the 1960s. Wilson, however, has always stressed that he was not essentially a drifter, and he has emphasized the unromantic aspects of the drifting life.[21] Beneath his apparent vagaries, his life during these years was given consistency by the quest for spiritual development that he conducted through reading, thinking and writing. But with his formal education over, and with sporadic and usually uneasy contact with any kind of intellectual community, he was to be forced more than ever to create his own context, his own mapping of reality.[22] Thus his intellectual development was to take a highly individual course: a course that was, nevertheless, to make a great appeal to his age when its fruits were made public in *The Outsider*.

After leaving school, Wilson worked in a Leicester wool factory while he studied for the maths exam he had to retake to get the five credits needed for matriculation. At this time, he was thinking of getting a job where he could study for a B.Sc. The financial position of his family made full-time study out of the question. The boredom of factory work stimulated him to read and write in the evenings; he worked on short stories and a long play, and read a lot of poetry. It was in this period that he decided to become, not a scientist, but a writer whose 'lifelong task would be to investigate the problem of the meaning of human existence'.[23] In two months, he gained the maths credit, and returned to his old school as a laboratory assistant. There was only one problem: he had lost all interest in science.

In view of this, it was hardly surprising that he proved an unsatisfactory employee. But in other ways, the year he spent in the job was significant. He continued to write, producing many short stories and plays, though he stopped submitting them after constant rejections. He also began keeping a journal: this was to prove an invaluable means of expressing and developing his feelings and ideas, and an important source of material for his early books, both fiction and non-fiction. To some extent, the journal compensated for his intellectual isolation, and it could be said that, in keeping it, he was serving his apprenticeship as a writer. He did much reading. He already knew much of T. S. Eliot, and he came to know most of Shaw's plays by heart. He read Dickens's *Pickwick Papers*, and this became the chief influence on the style of his short stories, though one he vehemently repudiated in his later work. He read Joyce's *Ulysses* and hated it; it seemed to reflect the triviality and ugliness he perceived all around him; but its careful naturalistic details, its stream-of-consciousness technique, and its 'mythic method' were important influences on the early versions of his first published novel. He discovered a compilation of religious texts called *The Bible of the World*, and responded especially to the *Tao Te Ching*, which seemed to reinforce the feeling of futility that still weighed on him.

His dislike of his job aggravated this feeling. Constant cerebration made things even worse. His discovery of the theories of Berkeley and Hume, in a textbook of philosophy, compounded a sense of futility with a near-solipsist feeling of the unreality of anything outside himself. Once, he suffered an acute 'vastation'; on another occasion, he contemplated suicide.

It would have been easy; he had access to hydrocyanic acid in the school laboratory. But when it came to the point of drinking it, he 'was suddenly supremely aware that what [he] wanted was not less life, but more'.[24] It was an intense affirmative experience, the opposite of the 'vastation'.

He was sacked as a laboratory assistant when he failed the end-of-year exams. He moved to a post as a clerk in the Leicester Tax Office, but there too he did not do well. Outside work, however, he began to make friends: one introduced him to Nijinsky's *Diary*, and to the life and work of Van Gogh. Both Nijinsky and Van Gogh assumed considerable importance in Wilson's personal mythology: they made prominent appearances in *The Outsider*, and contributed to the characterization of Austin Nunne and Oliver Glasp in *Ritual in the Dark*.

To his disgust, after a year in the Tax Office, Wilson passed the exam to become an established civil servant. He was transferred to another Tax Office in Rugby, home of the famous public school, a quiet town nineteen miles from Leicester. In Rugby public library, which he found far better than the one in Leicester, he studied *Finnegans Wake*. He also studied painting and sculpture in encyclopaedias of art lent to him by the Leicester friend who had introduced him to Van Gogh and Nijinsky. One evening, he went to see Bizet's *Carmen* at a theatre in the nearby town of Coventry. By then, he had been listening to concerts on B.B.C. Radio for years, but operas on the radio had bored him; the impact of a live performance of *Carmen* was, however, overwhelming. Here was one of the traditional cultural awakenings.

Wilson was called up in 1949 for National Service in the R.A.F. It looked like a two-year trap: but six months later, he was free. He was discharged after claiming to have homosexual tendencies. The claim was totally unfounded; Wilson was to be one of the first 'gay deceivers', a type that became widespread in America at the time of the Vietnam war. It was an unexpected liberation, and it confirmed the optimism that was starting to re-emerge, in a deepened form, from the sense of futility which had dominated his early teens. He resolved not to work in an office again; instead he found jobs on a building site, a fairground, and a farm. None lasted very long. He stopped reading Eliot for a time, declaring him 'morbid' and 'anti-life'.[25] Instead he had frequent recourse to Nietzsche's *Thus Spake Zarathustra*, Whitman's poems, and a condensation of *The Bible of the World* called *The Pocket World Bible*. He read Buddhist and Hindu texts for the first time, and the *Bhagavad Gita* became especially important to him.

In September 1950, he went to Paris, then to Strasbourg. Travelling gave him a feeling of freedom, but with little money, it was demoralizing. By the time he returned to Leicester in December, he was so pleased to be home that he took a clerical job again, this time in a steel works. But this quickly bored him, and he found work as a navvy with Leicester Corporation. This fell through too when he was not allowed to work part-time. He then found a fairly agreeable job at a chemical works.

In June 1951, he married, and set out alone to London to find a home for himself and his wife. She joined him soon afterwards. The books he chose to take with him to, as he put it, 'counteract bewilderment or loss of motive' give an interesting insight into his reading at this time. They were Blake, *The Pocket World Bible*, *Ulysses*, *London Book of Verse*, *Oxford Greek Verse*, Nietzsche, Eliot's poems, Dostoevsky's *House of the Dead* and *Brothers Karamazov*, and Dante's *Inferno*.[26]

The London in which the 19-year-old Wilson arrived is evoked by a writer with whom he was closely associated at the time of *The Outsider*, Stuart Holroyd:

> [It was] a city recovering from war. It was scarred and dingy and there were still extensive bomb sites. Rubble, greyness, smog, poverty, garish whores on the streets in Soho, trams still running along Kingsway, tramps sleeping on the Embankment and under the Arches: it was a run-down city by today's standards, but . . . it was [also] romantic and exciting.[27]

It was a London where one could live cheaply and find, in cafés, milkbars, pubs and on the streets, a variety of aspiring writers and artists, eccentrics, drifters and petty crooks. Young people of intelligence, who would be absorbed into the universities in the 1960s, came to this city to make their own way. It is a city which has vanished now, but which comes alive in the pages of Wilson's first two novels—especially *Adrift in Soho*.

Wilson's first eighteen months in London were no bohemian idyll, however. They consisted of factory jobs and some

months on the dole, constant changes of address due to accom-
modation problems, and the extra difficulties caused by the
arrival of a baby son. Nevertheless, marriage provided him
with a sense of emotional security that stimulated him to write.
He worked on a novel about two 'Outsiders', one based on
Nietzsche, the other on Jack the Ripper: here was the genesis
of *Ritual in the Dark*. In North Finchley public library, he
discovered the *Egyptian Book of the Dead* and studied it carefully, with the idea of using it as a structuring and symbolic
device for his fiction, as Joyce had used the *Odyssey* for *Ulysses*.

After eighteen difficult months, Wilson's wife moved with
their young son back to Leicester. It was to be a temporary
separation until Wilson found a permanent home for them all,
but it lengthened out indefinitely. Wilson worked for a time as
a hospital porter in Fulham, living in. Then he went to Paris
again, where he tried, unsuccessfully, to make a living by
selling subscriptions for literary magazines. Back in Leicester
once more for Christmas, he found work as a temporary shop
assistant at a big store in the city; there he met Joy Stewart,
who later became his second wife. In the new year, he returned
to London and worked in quick succession at a laundry, a
garage, a wine company, and a plastics factory. Four unsatisfactory jobs in four months made him decide upon the way of
life that was to become famous: spending his nights out of doors
in a sleeping bag on Hampstead Heath, and his days writing in
the British Museum Reading Room.

In the Reading Room, he worked hard on *Ritual in the Dark*.
When he had finished the first part, he gave it to the novelist
Angus Wilson to read. Angus Wilson was then Deputy Superintendent of the Reading Room; he had noticed Wilson writing,
and offered to look at his work. With the novel temporarily off
his hands, Wilson felt at a loose end. When he saw the manu-
script of Stuart Holroyd's literary and philosophical study,
Emergence from Chaos, he decided to write a similar book based on
his own ideas. 'I would dash it off quickly, and then get back to
the novel.'[28] The book that he dashed off was to be published
before the novel on which he had worked for years, and was to
make him famous. It was, of course, *The Outsider*.

The reception of *The Outsider* is a significant moment in the
history and sociology of twentieth-century English culture. A

17

detailed analysis of that reception is not the purpose of this study: the main points can be noted, however. At first, both the book and its author had enormous appeal. In the early 1950s, British cultural life had come under the influence of the 'Movement', a loosely defined group of poets and novelists who emphasized reason, caution and moderation. As one of their chief spokesmen, the poet Donald Davie, put it: 'A neutral tone is nowadays preferred.'[29] The 'Movement' drew strength from longstanding conservative traditions in English culture; but it offered nothing, was indeed in reaction against, the powerful current of English Romanticism, which stretched from Blake to the 'New Romantic' poets of the 1940s. In May 1956, that current dramatically re-emerged, with the opening of John Osborne's play *Look Back in Anger*, and the publication of *The Outsider*: both had strong Romantic appeal. The 'Movement' had stressed, had taken a pride in, the insularity of English culture: *The Outsider* offered a dashing introduction to a wide range of European thinkers and ideas. But in this it was, paradoxically, a boost to insularity; it seemed to show, in a period of national decline, that an Englishman could do as well as the Europeans.[30]

The Outsider also appealed, of course, to the young. In 1956, young people were starting to emerge from the grey chrysalis of the immediate post-war decade, but a distinctive youth sub-culture was only just beginning to develop, affluence was not yet widespread, and the new universities had not yet opened. For all these reasons, young people felt displaced: *The Outsider* seemed to explain and justify their position.

The appeal of the book was complemented by the appeal of its author—or, rather, of the legend that quickly grew up around him. Like John Osborne, he was billed as an 'Angry Young Man', raging against the torpor of '50s Britain.[31] As Martin Green has pointed out, Wilson was also seen as a new incarnation of an old mythological figure in European culture: he was a *Sonnenkind*, a 'Child of the Sun', young, glamorous, talented, male. Furthermore, he was from the working class, and had not been to a university: thus he especially appealed to those, often from privileged backgrounds themselves, who were drawn to the *Sonnenkind* myth, but held liberal political views.[32] Wilson was the token example of what a working-class boy

18

could achieve, a *Sonnenkind* of the people. He made a more general appeal to those, from a variety of backgrounds, who felt British society to be oppressive, class-conscious, and constricting; it seemed that, in Martin Green's words, 'somebody without any of the required training and manner had broken through into the closed circle.'[33]

Moreover, in 1956, the mass media, especially T.V., were starting to assume the enormous influence that they have in our lives today. For a short period, Wilson was to become a 'media intellectual', a vaunted 'thinker' who was also a 'personality'. In Wilson's case, the 'personality' counted for more than the 'thinker'; his distinctive appearance, and colourful life story made an immediate impact. As Kenneth Allsop remarked:

> With an ease that must have been the envy of all the copywriters in the country, he established what is called in the trade 'high brand-remembrance'.[34]

His youth meant that he also acquired something of a 'pop-star' charisma. Although he called it 'extraordinary' that his fame 'should have corresponded with that of James Dean, Elvis Presley, Bill Haley, Lonnie Donegan', it was not, in fact, so surprising.[35] Combining the appeal of the popularizing intellectual, the media personality, and the pop-star, Wilson became, briefly, one of the first *gurus* of post-war culture.

Wilson's reputation crashed as quickly as it had grown. Once again, the reasons are manifold. Wilson did not conform to the values of the liberal intelligentsia who had taken him up at first; he was perceived, not wholly without justification, as immodest and arrogant; his emphasis on the Will, his praise of Sir Oswald Mosley, and his involvement with a short-lived political party called the Spartacans led to him being denounced as a fascist. *The Outsider*, on closer examination, seemed to be less good than it had looked at first. There was adverse publicity about his personal life: a newspaper story about his first marriage, then a blaze of publicity when the father of Joy Stewart tried to horsewhip him.

All this made Wilson decide to settle in Cornwall. He has lived there since 1957. He married Joy Stewart, and has remained firmly attached to her and their children. Apart from lecture tours and temporary teaching posts in America, he has been a full-time writer. From 1957, the story of his life has become, largely, the story of his books. This, Wilson would claim, is the story that really counts.

In Cornwall, he has been able to compensate massively for the cultural deprivation of his childhood, by writing energetically, and by indulging his passions for books and music and ideas. His thinking has developed in a number of interesting ways, and he has made many discoveries in his reading, but he has also stayed remarkably loyal to the major influences of his early years. Shaw still holds the highest place in his pantheon, and he continues to regard Wells as a key figure, though he now admires his later novels above his early science fiction. He has also retained a loyalty to the sensation literature of his boyhood; this shows itself in his novels.

Wilson worked on stoically through the 1960s, keeping up a regular flow of fiction and non-fiction. Money was tight, and he felt badly treated by critics. Although he has sometimes exaggerated their ill-treatment, in the interests of a heroic self-image, it is true that his work was rarely discussed seriously. In response, Wilson's tendency to dogmatic self-assertion in his writing and press interviews increased, and he developed a habit of ignoring even valid criticism.

With the publication of *The Occult* in 1971, however, he began to find a new audience, especially among those who had grown up under the influence of the 'counter-culture' of the later '60s. He also began to find more critical acceptance. But he is still, essentially, a 'fringe' figure. Though he puts in a claim for his centrality, he also seems to think his marginal position inevitable. Perhaps he even prefers it.

Wilson is, nonetheless, representative in his difference. His life has taken him through a series of situations which exemplify major features of culture and society in twentieth-century Britain. The culturally deprived working-class background; the voyage through the 'lower depths' of post-war Britain; the spectacular leap to success through the power of mass communications, a power as dangerous and unstable as nuclear energy; rejection, derision, and neglect, reinforcing cultural isolation; and a slow working back to an established position. Throughout all this, because of all this, Wilson has had to create his own cultural context, using the materials to hand. To do this is to make one's own mapping of reality, and ultimately, if one is driven by metaphysical needs as Wilson is, of the universe. Wilson may seem eccentric: in this, he is central. He has carried out, in an explicit and sustained way, an activity which anyone who reflects upon his life in depth, and has a hunger for seriousness, must carry out today, in our age of cultural pluralism, fragmentation, and debasement. He has made his own world, for the lack of any other.

We must know the broad outlines of that world to understand Wilson's fiction. Like the novels of Wells and the plays of Shaw, his fiction takes its place in the total world which its author has created, in the comprehensive structuring of existence which Wilson has conducted through his studies of philosophy, psychology, sexuality, murder, the occult, and literature. We shall now turn to these.

NOTES

1. J. B. Priestley, *English Journey* (Heinemann & Gollancz, 1934), pp. 118–19. The journey Priestley describes actually took place in Autumn, 1933.
2. This is the figure given in C. Wilson *Voyage to a Beginning* (Woolf, 1969), p. 12.
3. The adjective 'cultural' refers here to traditional 'high' culture—literature, classical music, ballet, theatre, painting, sculpture—and to the aspect of 'popular' culture fed by the language of the Authorized Version of the Bible and the Book of Common Prayer. This is not to deny that an urban working-class family in the 1930s and '40s may have partaken in a distinctive culture of its own, if we broaden the concept of culture to include a whole way of life, with its traditions and values. See Richard Hoggart, *The Uses of Literacy* (Chatto & Windus, 1957).
4. *Voyage*, p. 9.
5. *Uses of Literacy* (my ref. to Pelican, 1977 ed.), pp. 138–39.
6. *Voyage*, p. 18.
7. *Voyage*, p. 12.
8. *Voyage*, p. 12.
9. *Voyage*, p. 47. In his published work, Wilson first uses the term 'vastation' in *The Outsider* (Gollancz, 1956; my refs. to Picador, 1978 ed.), p. 123. He derives it from William James Sr., who took it in turn from Swedenborg. For Wilson, the term denotes a devastation, a laying waste, of all values and meanings.
10. *Voyage*, pp. 26–7.
11. *Voyage*, p. 35.

12. C. Wilson, 'Personal. Influences on my Writing' in his *Eagle and Earwig* (John Baker, 1965), p. 271.

13. Even for a child brought up on 'high' culture, 'popular' literature can still be a vital imaginative stimulus. See Jean-Paul Sartre's account of how it provided him with 'some *genuine* reading' during his childhood, although he was surrounded by 'classic' books: *Words*, trans. by Irene Clephane (Penguin, 1967), pp. 47–9.

14. H. G. Wells, *Experiment in Autobiography* (Gollancz & The Cresset Press, 1934), 2 vols., I, p. 168.

15. C. Wilson, *Religion and the Rebel* (Gollancz, 1957), p. 15.

16. *Voyage*, p. 41; *Eagle and Earwig*, p. 271.

17. *Eagle and Earwig*, p. 267.

18. Asa Briggs, *Sound and Vision*, vol. IV of *The History of Broadcasting in the United Kingdom* (O.U.P., 1979), p. 65.

19. 'Prefatory Note', *The Philosopher's Stone* (Barker, 1969; my refs. to Panther, 1974 ed.), p. 5.

20. *Voyage*, p. 36.

21. *Voyage*, p. 112. *Religion and Rebel*, p. 30. See also Wilson's comments on Hermann Hesse's romanticization of the wandering life in *Hesse, Reich, Borges* (Village Press, 1974).

22. While working in the Leicester Tax Office, Wilson joined a Drama Group, and attended evening classes, at a local college (*Voyage*, pp. 49–50). On his first visit to Paris, he stayed at a kind of Rousseau-esque 'Akademia' run by Raymond Duncan, but left after a few weeks (*Voyage*, pp. 78–9; *Religion and Rebel*, pp. 30–1). In London, he had some association with Alfred Reynolds's 'Bridge' group (C. Wilson, 'On the Bridge', *Encounter*, April 1960, pp. 17–24), the London Anarchist Group, and the Syndicalist Workers' Federation of North London (*Voyage*, pp. 86–9; Sidney Campion, *The World of Colin Wilson*, Muller, 1963, pp. 106–9). The community formed by himself, Stuart Holroyd, and Bill Hopkins around the time of *The Outsider* was the one in which he felt most at home, but that did not survive, though friendship remained. Essentially, however, Wilson has always been a loner, who is not inclined to co-operative or communal activity.

23. *Voyage*, p. 43.

24. *Religion and Rebel*, p. 25.

25. *Religion and Rebel*, p. 28.

26. *World of Colin Wilson*, p. 102.

27. Stuart Holroyd, *Contraries* (Bodley Head, 1975), p. 21. Holroyd is describing London in Autumn, 1952, but his description would certainly fit London in the previous year.

28. *Religion and Rebel*, p. 38.

29. Blake Morrison, *The Movement* (O.U.P., 1980).

30. In this respect, it is significant that Philip Toynbee, in his *Observer* review of *The Outsider*, compared Wilson, favourably, with Sartre. *Voyage*, p. 122.

31. The picture is complicated, of course, by the fact that at least two writers associated with the 'Movement'—Kingsley Amis and John Wain—were

also billed as 'Angry Young Men' (cf. Peter Lewis, *The Fifties*, Heinemann, 1978, p. 160). Compared to Wilson and Osborne, however, these were not newcomers: John Wain's first novel appeared in 1953, Amis's in 1954.

32. Martin Green, *Children of the Sun* (Constable, 1977), p. 460.

33. Martin Green, *A Mirror for Anglo-Saxons* (Cape, 1961), p. 62. It should be said that this was Green's attitude before he read *The Outsider*. When he did so, he decided it was 'very bad'.

34. Kenneth Allsop, *The Angry Decade* (Peter Owen, 1957), p. 166. The section of this book called 'The Law Givers' contains the best account so far of Wilson's impact in the '50s. Now, however, with the benefit of hindsight, a more comprehensive account could be written.

35. Extract from Wilson's journal, first published in *Daily Mail*, quoted in Christopher Booker, *The Neophiliacs* (Collins, 1969), p. 111.

2

Evolutionary Existentialism

Gerard Sorme, the hero-narrator of Wilson's novel *The God of the Labyrinth* calls himself an 'evolutionary existentialist'.[1] The term could equally well apply to Wilson himself. It sums up the two major strands which meet in his thought, but their fusion may seem rather surprising. The vitalist evolutionary doctrine that Wilson endorses has had little influence since the First World War. It seems to us today like the last, desperate fling of nineteenth-century optimism. After 1918, it has had, at least before Colin Wilson, only two major advocates: Bernard Shaw and Teilhard de Chardin. Shaw's claim that 'Creative Evolution . . . is . . . unmistakeably the religion of the twentieth century' does not seem to have been justified, however.[2] Neither has de Chardin's attempt to fuse the evolutionary vision with Catholic Christianity proved especially convincing.[3]

Existentialism seems much more of our time. Like Creative Evolution, it can be linked with religion: Kierkegaard, often regarded as the founder of existentialism in the nineteenth century, was a Christian, and, in our own century, Paul Tillich has tried to create an 'existential theology'. But existentialism has become best known in our time in its non-Christian version, identified above all with Jean-Paul Sartre. In contrast to Creative Evolution, this version of existentialism is pessimistic, emphasizing alienation, defeat, and despair. In Sartre's famous formulation: 'Man is a useless passion.'[4] It offers only stoicism—and social and political commitment—as an antidote.

Wilson rejects this pessimism: he claims that evolutionary optimism is more than ever justified today; that man is on the verge of a breakthrough into a higher state, a new evolutionary phase:

> The prophets of decadence and the 'decline of the West' were wrong. We are living in one of the most important epochs in human history.[5]

To support this belief, however, Wilson turns to existentialism, insofar as its method is to focus upon the moments of individual human experience. On the basis of his analysis of such moments, he attacks what he terms the 'passive fallacy' in Western philosophy—the concept of man as an empty consciousness that passively receives data from the outside world. This concept was expressed by, for example, the English empiricist philosopher John Locke, when he compared the mind to 'white paper, void of all characters'.[6] Within existentialism itself, it is the view taken by Sartre.[7] To refute this view, Wilson draws upon the theory of perception put forward by the German philosopher, Edmund Husserl.

Husserl is generally regarded as the founding father of the discipline called phenomenology. Wilson defines this as 'the study of the way that consciousness perceives objects'.[8] For Wilson, the core of Husserl's theory is his view that man's consciousness plays an active role in perception; that it is, in Husserl's terminology, 'intentional'. The meaning of what we observe is not automatically given to us; we have to direct and focus our consciousness in order to perceive it. Wilson endorses Husserl's belief that this perceptual process is carried out by a 'Transcendental Ego', an 'I' over and above the 'I' of everyday consciousness.

Wilson emphasizes, however, that although we have to play an active role in the perception of meaning, we do not create meaning: meaning is constituted by a web of relationships that have an independent existence. But normally, we perceive only a small part of these relationships:

> The web is already there, stretching in all directions, but for the most part, it is in darkness; only a tiny area around 'me' is illuminated. My sense of 'significances' is entirely dependent upon the size of the illuminated area.[9]

To expand our perception of meaning, of the web of relationships, beyond a certain limit, we have to move beyond immediate sense-data, although such data may continue to be significantly involved in our perception. Wilson suggests that such a movement is fuelled by an apprehension—not a mere intellectual awareness—of realities other than those of immediate sense-data. He attributes this apprehension to a special faculty, which he calls 'Faculty X':

> Faculty X is the key to all poetic and mystical experience. . . . [It] is simply the latent power human beings possess *to reach beyond the present*. After all, we know perfectly well that the past is as real as the present, and that New York and Singapore and Lhasa and Stepney Green are all as real as this place I happen to be in at the moment. *Yet my senses do not agree.* They assure me that this place, here and now, is far more real than any other place or any other time. Only in certain moments of great inner intensity do I know this to be a lie. Faculty X is a sense of reality, the reality of other places and other times.[10]

Clearly, there is a distinction between the reality of a place which we believe to exist at the present time, but which is not accessible to our senses, and the reality of the past. There is a further distinction between the reality of our own past, and that of the non-personal past, the past of history. In Wilson's view, however, what divides them is less important than what they have in common: the fact that, while they cannot, by definition, be experienced as immediate sense-data, we can nevertheless have an experience of them which is characterized by our conviction of their reality. It may be said that this experience can be attributed to imagination or memory operating at a certain level of intensity. Wilson distinguishes, however, between experiences attributed to imagination or memory which are not characterized by the conviction that they enforce of their reality (and Wilson would claim that these are most of our imaginative and recollective experiences) and experiences attributed to imagination or memory which do enforce such a conviction. These two forms of experience are different, not only in degree, but in kind. To assimilate them both to imagination or memory would be to suppress this difference.

Faculty X, by enabling us to experience realities other than those of sense-data, expands our perception of meaning, of the web of relationships between this place and that, now and ten years ago. The realities that we experience need not be spatial or temporal, however; they may be of a philosophical or mathematical nature. There are certainly distinctions between all these entities; but, once more, they are united by the conviction that they enforce of their reality: a reality which is other than that of sense-data, which has an independent existence, and which is not experienced in the usual operations of imagination, memory, or intellection.

Perception of such realities and of the web of meaning that they entail can expand to such an extent that it becomes what has traditionally been called a 'mystical experience'. Wilson has given many examples of these in his non-fiction; here is an especially clear one that he quotes from William James:

> I seemed all at once to be reminded of a past experience; and this reminiscence, ere I could conceive or name it distinctly, developed into something further that belonged with it, this in turn into something further still, and so on, until the process faded out, leaving me amazed at the sudden vision of increasing ranges of distant facts of which I could give no articulate account. The mode of consciousness was perceptual, not conceptual—the field expanding so fast that there seemed no time for conception or identification to get in its work. There was a strongly exciting sense that my knowledge of past (or present?) reality was enlarging pulse by pulse. . . . The feeling—I won't call it belief—that I had had a sudden *opening*, had seen through a window, as it were, into distant realities that incomprehensibly belonged with my own life, was so acute that I cannot shake it off today.[11]

Wilson does not believe that such experiences should be only occasional and unexpected; they should be available to human beings whenever they want them. They are man's natural birthright.

Wilson distinguishes, however, between two broad kinds of expanded perception: active and passive. He argues that the active kind, which involves a heightened sense of power and purpose as well as of meaning, is the more important. An experience of meaning alone may produce only quiescence, a sense that 'nothing matters', which contradicts the evolutionary

27

imperative. Such an experience will also, in Wilson's terms, be weaker since he sees meaning and purpose as bound up together, meaning generating purpose, purpose generating meaning.

Wilson affirms that, if we could gain constant access to our 'Transcendental Egos', we could control our 'intentionality', control the way that we perceive reality, and thus enjoy the active kind of expanded perception at will. Once we could do this, we would have reached the next stage in human evolution. Our increased sense of reality, meaning, power, and purpose would not only mean that we lived permanently on a higher level: it would also make possible greatly increased lifespan, and far more control over our 'luck', our physical and mental health, and over those powers, such as telepathy and psycho-kinesis, that we now call 'occult'.

At present, however, we cannot enjoy the active kind of expanded perception at will: the spirit bloweth where it listeth. For Wilson, it is one of the ironic facts of human nature that such perception, while it often deserts us in comfortable cir-cumstances, can be stirred by discomfort or crisis. He frequently cites the incident towards the end of Graham Greene's novel *The Power and the Glory* (1940), where the whisky-priest, about to be executed, feels that 'it would have been quite easy to be a saint.'[12] This exemplifies Wilson's axiom that:

> human beings can lapse into a mood of indifference where pleasure has no power to stimulate, and where only active discomfort or pain can penetrate the boredom.[13]

Wilson would further contend that, even if the whisky-priest had, like Dostoevsky, enjoyed a last-minute reprieve, he might easily have lapsed back into the old indifference, with the vision of sainthood, of enormous potential, disappearing. Wilson calls this failure to recognize, in comfortable circum-stances, the value of life, the 'St Neot margin' or the 'indiffer-ence margin', and suggests that this may be what is meant by Original Sin. The 'St Neot margin' provides Wilson with an explanation of the deliberate pursuit of suffering and danger by some 'Outsiders', such as Van Gogh, T. E. Lawrence, and Ernest Hemingway.[14]

It is possible to approach the active kind of expanded perception by less painful and destructive means—through sex, through meditation, through intellectual and creative activity. Such methods do not always work, however; and they often depend upon immediate external stimuli. Wilson believes that this haphazard state of affairs is the major obstacle to evolution. What is needed is the ability to enjoy active expanded perception at any appropriate time, even in the virtual absence of external stimuli, for example in a 'black room', the lightproof, soundproof room developed by American scientists for sensory deprivation experiments on humans. The 'black room' is an important symbol for Wilson.

Wilson has developed an analysis of the factors which, in his view, affect the capacity of human consciousness to achieve active expanded perception. He draws upon experiments in brain physiology which have suggested that the two halves of the cerebral cortex have different functions. Wilson contends that the left half of the brain deals with the everyday world: it is responsible for language, rational and critical thinking, the sense of time and space, and the personal ego. The right half of the brain looks inward: it has little capacity for language or rational and critical thinking, and is less aware of time, space, and the personal ego. It can, however, make us aware of overall patterns and meanings, of the web of relationships extending beyond sense-data. In other words, the right-brain plays a major role in producing both the active and passive kinds of expanded perception.

Western civilization has emphasized left-brain perception at the expense of the right. The East has emphasized right-brain perception at the expense of the left. In the twentieth century in the West, there has been a reaction against the left-brain bias. We see it, for example, in Freud's characterization of the ego as repressive, and D. H. Lawrence's rejection of 'head-consciousness'; in the decline of the moral vocabulary of will, self-discipline, and effort; in the growing interest, especially in recent years, in Asiatic religions, and in meditation and relaxation techniques. Wilson, in line with his preference for active rather than passive expanded perception, feels that this reaction, while valid up to a point, runs the risk of rejecting the left-brain too completely, of swinging to the opposite extreme. He suggests that the best technique is to combine the functions of the right and left brains in order to produce the active kind of expanded perception. It may be, Wilson says, this combination that constitutes 'Faculty X'. He proposes that 'psychologically . . . we consist of three major components: the left-brain, the right-brain, and the "robot".' He feels that the robot is probably located in the cerebellum—the small, posterior part of the brain.[17]

The 'robot' is a major obstacle to expanded perception. In defining this concept, one example Wilson gives is that of learning to drive. At first, it is necessary for the learner to think consciously about such operations as steering, changing gear, and braking; after a time, he finds himself performing all these operations without having to think consciously about them. A 'robot' has taken over. Wilson comments:

> This robot is a labour-saving device. . . . When an activity has been performed often enough, he takes it over, and what is more, he does it a great deal more efficiently than I could do it consciously. . . . [But the robot] has taken over too many of our functions.[16]

The 'robot' may, for example, take over when we listen to music or make love, and then these activities will fail to produce expanded perception. Fresh external stimuli—a new L.P. or mistress, for instance—may temporarily put the 'robot' out of action; but this is only a short-term expedient.

In defeating the robot, Wilson stresses the importance of the will. He distinguishes between two kinds of will: the kind which can be ineffective or counter-productive, as we may will in vain to stop worrying, or with the result that we worry more; and the truly potent will. In Wilson's model of brain physiology, the first kind of will would be due to the left brain working without sufficient support from the right, while the second kind would be due to the left and right brains working in combination.

Wilson also emphasizes the necessity of effort and self-discipline. In his stress on the will, effort, and self-discipline, he employs a moral vocabulary which is rather out of fashion today. His evolutionary ethics bear some resemblance to the Victorian gospel of hard work and self-help. He is even fond of comparing the will to a muscle which, like any muscle, can be strengthened by exercise; terms like 'flabby' and 'short-winded' are applied as pejorative adjectives to mental states. It seems at times that Wilson is offering an evolutionary existentialist alternative to Muscular Christianity.

He sees optimism and cheerfulness as very important as well. In this, he calls to mind what William James called the 'mind-cure' techniques that became popular, especially in America, in the later nineteenth century: Christian Science is the best-known version of these.[17] In the twentieth century, such techniques have been given best-selling expression by Norman Vincent Peale in books like *The Power of Positive Thinking*.[18]

Wilson would like human beings to achieve the functional efficiency of machines. Technology is the most abundant source of his imagery for human beings in both his fiction and non-fiction. He is especially fond of comparing people to cars or parts of them—engines, gears, accelerators, tyres, batteries, headlights, chokes—but radio sets, clocks and watches, neon lights, searchlights, record players, radar, hovercrafts, guns, microscopes, and hosiery machines have all supplied him with images of man. Human beings are 'miserably inefficient machines', and we need a 'science of human engineering'. It should be possible to get the mind into gear, or find the volume control knob which will turn up consciousness.[19] Wilson's fondness for such imagery is due, in part, to his desire to avoid 'the mystical vagaries of some writers on "cosmic consciousness".'[20] Perhaps it also owes something to his upbringing in an industrial town, his education at a Technical School, and his factory jobs.[21] Most twentieth-century writers have set themselves against technology in their work; Wilson, like Marinetti and the Futurists, seems to welcome it. He sings the man who holds the steering wheel, but the steering wheel is internalized.[22] In contrast to those visual artists of the twentieth century who have, in their work, imitated the appearance of machines but subverted their function, Wilson stresses the function of machines, their efficiency.[23]

To sum up: men will have reached the next evolutionary stage when they can enjoy active expanded perception at will. In working towards that stage, they must try and find ways of making the left and right halves of the brain work in combination, and they must gain control over the 'robot'. To

31

achieve these ends, they need to employ will, effort, and self-discipline, to maintain a high level of optimism, and to acquire the functional efficiency of machines.

From this central core of ideas, Wilson's interests extend into psychology, sexuality, murder, the occult, and literary criticism. We shall consider each of these in turn.

In his thinking on psychology, Wilson has been deeply influenced by the work of the American psychologist Abraham Maslow, who died in 1970. Maslow was an influential exponent of what has come to be called 'Humanistic Psychology'. He attacked the view that man's basic drives were sexual, aggressive, or self-destructive, and argued that his creative, idealistic and spiritual aspirations were equally fundamental. This naturally appealed to Wilson's evolutionary optimism. Maslow followed up a well-known objection to Freud: that Freud's model of human personality was distorted because it derived largely from studies of people defined as 'sick'. Maslow conducted studies of people whom he judged to be 'enormously healthy', who lead apparently fulfilling lives. He termed these 'self-actualizers'. He concluded that most 'self-actualizers' enjoy what he called 'peak experiences'. Wilson comments:

> The 'peak experience' is not necessarily a mystical experience although mystical experiences are one form of peak experience. A young mother watching her husband and children eat breakfast had a 'peak experience'; a hostess sitting alone in the room after a highly successful party had a 'peak experience'. It is a sense of life-affirmation of the kind that Proust described in *Swann's Way* when he wrote, 'I had ceased now to feel mediocre, accidental, mortal. . . .'[24]

The 'peak experience' is clearly due to an expanded perception of meaning, of the web of relationships. Maslow's researches support Wilson's belief in the capacity of the human mind to achieve such perception. But Wilson dissents from Maslow's view that the 'peak experience' cannot be summoned at will. He emphasizes, however, that the 'peak experience' is not an end in itself, but a spur to evolutionary effort, to finding a way of living permanently on the peaks.

Wilson has developed his interest in psychology in two specific areas: the psychology of sexuality, and of murder. The two are interrelated, since the kind of murder that most interests Wilson is the 'sex murder'. Let us look first at his attitude to sexuality. Wilson sees sex as an important and easily accessible means to active expanded perception. In his analysis of the sexual impulse, he puts forward a 'theory of symbolic response'. The human sexual response, he argues, is produced by the imagination utilizing and directing sexual energy. The imagination responds to symbols. These symbols are not, as Freud would suggest, symbols of the sexual organs: they are symbols of intensity. For the human male, the most exciting sexual symbols are those which stand for the alien and the forbidden, because they promise a greater intensity. This is why, in Wilson's view, a sudden, unexpected glimpse of a woman's underwear can be more exciting than a naked and willing woman. Sexual perversion is an attempt to find more intense symbols of the alien and forbidden.

To concentrate upon sex in the quest for intensity is, however, a fundamental misdirection of a desire which is essentially evolutionary, and which can only find sustained satisfaction when directed to evolutionary ends. The attempt to satisfy it through sex is bound to be disappointing in the end, since it is primarily an imaginative rather than a sexual desire.

The ultimate misdirection of the quest for intensity is murder. Wilson does not apply this to all murders; he acknowledges that many are committed for reasons of material gain or need, or from motives such as anger and hatred; but he argues that the advance of civilization has produced a new kind of murderer who kills, not for the traditional motives, but for the excitement that killing generates in him. Very often, such murders are linked with sexual assault and deviant sexual practices. Wilson rejects the concept of 'diminished responsibility' in such cases, or the view that they are primarily due to psychopathic or genetic disorders. He contends that they spring from a deliberate act of choice: they are committed by those who seek a greater intensity, whose imagination and will-to-power are frustrated, but who lack the intelligence and self-discipline to find a creative means of self-realization: a means that would turn their desire for intensity in an evolutionary direction. Murder is a profoundly anti-evolutionary act. The negation of values and the lowering of self-esteem that it necessarily entails mean that, in the end, the murderer's energies, his desire for intensity, will be even more frustrated. He stands self-condemned before any judge and jury can condemn him.

From the dark area of murder, we come to another murky region of Wilson's interests: the occult. In recent years, there has been an enormous upsurge of interest in such matters as alchemy, astral travelling, astrology, chiromancy, clairvoyance, divination, dowsing, geomancy, ghosts, life after death, poltergeists, psychic healing, psychokinesis, psychometry, reincarnation, scrying, spontaneous combustion, telepathy, and witchcraft. On one view, the occult provides evidence of man's hidden powers, and of the fact that the universe is far richer and stranger than our day-to-day perception would suggest. The opposite view holds that it demonstrates only the human capacity for self-delusion. Wilson once held this view: he felt that the occult was a 'poetic fiction, a symbol of the world that *ought* to exist but didn't. In short, wishful thinking.' His researches have convinced him, however, that 'the basic claims of "occultism" are true': man does have 'strange powers' such as telepathy and psychokinesis; the 'reality of life after death has been established beyond all reasonable doubt'; the existence of various kinds of 'spirit entities' is a real possibility.[25]

Wilson has stressed however that he does not consider himself an 'occultist' because he is 'more interested in the mechanisms of everyday consciousness'.[26] He endeavours to incorporate occult phenomena into his general philosophical standpoint. It is clearly only a short step from belief in a 'Transcendental Ego' to belief in a 'soul' that survives death, and if one accepts that a 'soul' can exist outside the body, it is only a short further step to belief in other 'spirit entities'. Apparently paranormal powers such as telepathy and precognition can be attributed to contact with the web of relationships that extends beyond the everyday world and links us to other places and times, including the future. In terms of Wilson's model of brain physiology, the right side of the brain, which enables us to grasp overall patterns, is responsible for such powers. But at present most of us in the West, with its left-brain bias, are unaware that we possess such powers, and the small proportion of people who do seem to display them often cannot control them very well. Wilson believes that it should be possible to control them at will, as it should be possible to control the whole mode of consciousness. The man of the future, who can enjoy active expanded perception whenever he wants to, will also command powers now regarded as occult or non-existent.

Finally, let us consider Wilson's literary criticism. In this area, his central argument is for an 'existential criticism'. He endorses T. S. Eliot's dictum that 'literary criticism should be completed by criticism from a definite philosophical or theological standpoint.'[27] He argues that a literary work—novel, short story, play, poem—contains, implicitly at least, a world-view: a statement about the nature of reality. It is the task of the existential critic to bring this world-view into the open, and judge it according to its degree of correspondence with the evolutionary existentialist philosophy. If the world-view is pessimistic, seeing human life as futile, meaningless, or dominated by failure and suffering, this, in evolutionary existentialist terms, is a partial, distorted vision, a 'worm's-eye view', a libel on existence.

It is this world-view, however, that Wilson sees as dominant in twentieth-century literature. Often it is epitomized by the 'weak hero'—over-sensitive, ineffectual, self-pitying, lacking purpose—of many twentieth-century novels. This hero is typified for Wilson by Gumbril in Aldous Huxley's *Antic Hay*, who says: 'I glory in the name of earwig.'[28] Wilson largely rejects the idea that such pessimism is a reflection of the objective conditions of humanity in the twentieth century—the century of two world wars, of the mass murder of Jews, of the nuclear bomb. He asserts that 'it is not a question of modern life, but of the artist himself.'[29] The limitations of the world-view are the personal limitations of the writer. For example, the failure that Wilson perceives in D. H. Lawrence's work is attributed to the fact that Lawrence 'was spoiled by his mother, and encouraged to become imperious, fretful and self-pitying'.[30]

Wilson also attacks modernist and postmodernist work for its esotericism, and deplores the gap that has opened up in the twentieth century between serious and popular literature.

With these views, Wilson has made short work of some revered twentieth-century writers and works. *Finnegans Wake* is 'little more than an interesting rag-bag of linguistic experiments'[31]; D. H. Lawrence 'cannot be judged a great writer'[32]; Samuel Beckett may be dismissed as 'a case of arrested metaphysical growth'.[33] He has created a list of alternative admirations: the later novels of H. G. Wells, the *Voyage of Arcturus* of David Lindsay, the novels of John Cowper Powys and L. H. Myers, Bill Hopkins' *The Divine and the Decay*[34]: all these are works which, in Wilson's judgement, have attempted to take a larger, 'bird's-eye view' of life.

These, then, are the broad outlines of Wilson's world; they constitute the mapping of reality he has made for himself. We can say of it what we said of Wilson's life: that it is both eccentric and representative; representative in its eccentricity. There are a number of reasons for the 'fringe' status of Wilson's ideas: his ventures into such dubious areas as the study of murder and the occult; his heavy reliance on what he feels to be intuition; his lack of concern with scholarly discipline; his swagger and self-assertiveness in his writing, the Wilson *persona* that can alienate people as did Shaw's 'GBS' *persona*. These features also give him a certain following, and can be refreshing in our over-academicized age; but they inhibit wider acceptance.

Like many 'fringe' ideas that have developed in the twentieth century, those of Wilson can be seen, to some extent, as an attempt to find a substitute for traditional religion. We can reasonably accept Wilson's point that human beings are not neutral observers of the world, but that their perceptions of it are selective and biased—though it is questionable how far they are, or ever could be, in control of their perceptions, and how far those perceptions are dominated by the physiological, linguistic, social and political structures in which human beings exist. We can also accept that meditation and biofeedback techniques seem to suggest that a certain degree of control over consciousness, and thus over perception, is possible. For example, we may be able to train ourselves to relax more, and thus experience the world differently even in terms of sense-data; more relaxation could, in some cases, improve our physical health and perhaps even extend our lifespan by a few months or years. But to move from these propositions to an acceptance of the idea that sustained control of consciousness is possible, and that it will constitute an evolutionary breakthrough with all the consequences envisaged by Wilson, is to make a 'leap of faith' of milleniarian proportions. There seems little doubt that if Wilson was a more extroverted personality, he could become, like George Gurdjieff, the leader of a 'fringe' psychological-religious 'cult of unreason'.[35]

The concept of a 'fringe', however, demands the concept of a centre; and today things fall apart: the centre does not hold. It may be that it is on the 'fringe' that the new centres are being created: the centres for the future. 'Future' is the key word in considering Wilson. His work, both fiction and non-fiction, is an attempt to create a centre for the future. He looks both at existence—at man as he is now—and at evolution—at man's movement towards the future; a movement which is occurring all the time, even if not in the way Wilson sees it. His work constitutes an attempt at a re-definition of man in the light of the future. Such attempts are the necessary work of today.

Wilson sees his novels as playing a unique role in this re-definition:

> For me . . . [they] are a manner of philosophising. . . . Philosophy may be only a shadow of the reality it tries to grasp, but the novel is altogether more satisfactory. I am almost tempted to . . . say that no philosopher is qualified to do his job unless he is also a novelist. . . . Shaw once said he would have given any dozen of Shakespeare's plays for one of the prefaces he ought to have written. I would certainly exchange any of the works of Whitehead or Wittgenstein for the novels they ought to have written.[36]

We have explored the broad outlines of the world, the context, in which Wilson's novels have their place. We now need to focus more closely on his attitude to the novel.

NOTES

1. *The God of the Labyrinth* (Hart Davis, 1970; my refs. to Mayflower, 1974 ed.), p. 246.
2. Bernard Shaw, 'Preface: the Infidel Half Century' *Back to Methuselah* (1921, preface revd. 1944; my refs. to Penguin, 1954 ed.), p. 57.
3. For Wilson's comments on Teilhard de Chardin, see his *Beyond the Outsider* (Barker, 1965), pp. 132–33.
4. Jean-Paul Sartre, *Being and Nothingness*, trans. by Hazel Barnes (Methuen, 1957), p. 615.

5. C. Wilson, *Bernard Shaw: A Reassessment* (Hutchinson, 1969), p. 298.

6. John Locke, *An Essay Concerning Human Understanding* (O.U.P., 1975), p. 104. 'Paper' and 'Characters' capitalized in original.

7. Wilson has written a lot on Sartre, but on this point see especially *Beyond the Outsider* and *Introduction to the New Existentialism* (Hutchinson, 1966).

8. *Beyond the Outsider*, p. 84. Italics in original.

9. *Poetry and Mysticism* (Hutchinson, 1970), p. 61.

10. *The Occult* (Hodder & Stoughton, 1971; my refs. to Mayflower, 1973 ed.), pp. 73–4.

11. Quoted in *Intro to New Existm*, pp. 103–4. Wilson gives sources as *Journal of Philosophy, Psychology and Scientific Methods* (1910) and *The Psychedelic Review*, No. 5 (1965).

12. Graham Greene, *The Power and the Glory* (Heinemann, 1940; my ref. to Penguin, 1962 ed.), p. 210. Wilson often misquotes this as 'it would have been so easy to be a saint.'

13. *Voyage*, p. 7. Wilson relates how the notion came to him as he was passing through the town of St. Neots in Huntingdonshire—hence the name 'St Neot margin'.

14. All figures discussed in *Outsider*.

15. C. Wilson, *Frankenstein's Castle. The Double Brain: Door to Wisdom* (Ashgrove Press, 1980) deals with these ideas on brain physiology.

16. *Poetry and Mysticism*, pp. 38–9.

17. Cf. William James, *Varieties of Religious Experience* (Longmans, 1952), Lectures IV and V, 'The Religion of Healthy-Mindedness', pp. 92–124. James comments that 'mind-cure has developed a living system of mental hygiene. . . . This system is wholly compacted of optimism: "Pessimism leads to weakness. Optimism leads to power". . . . No one can fail of the regenerative influence of optimistic thinking, pertinaciously pursued. Every man owns indefeasibly this inlet to the divine. Fear, on the contrary, and all the contracted and egoistic modes of thought, are inlets to destruction.' James points out, however, that 'mind-cure' advocates relaxation of the will; Wilson exhorts us to strengthen the will.

18. In *The Mind Parasites* (Barker, 1967), the narrator actually says: 'My strength came from optimism, from "positive thinking"', although he calls 'positive thinking' 'that dubious phrase'.

19. Cf. *Man Without a Shadow* (Barker, 1963; my refs. to Granada, 1980 ed. as *The Sex Diary of Gerard Sorme*), p. 23 for 'miserably inefficient machines' and Epigraph One to *Beyond the Outsider*, where the phrase 'science of human engineering' is attributed to Gustav Neumann, a major character in *Necessary Doubt*, although Neumann does not use the phrase in that novel.

20. *Poetry and Mysticism*, p. 18.

21. In *Voyage*, p. 36, Wilson relates how a lot of his time at school was spent in the College of Art and Technology, and there were classes in hosiery, engineering, and boots-and-shoes.

22. Cf. F. T. Marinetti, 'The Joy of Mechanical Force', from the 'Manifesto of Futurism', trans. by Eugen Weber, in R. Ellman and C. Feidelson Jr.

eds., *The Modern Tradition: Backgrounds of Modern Literature* (O.U.P., New York, 1965), pp. 431–35, esp. p. 433: 'We want to sing the man who holds the steering wheel.'

23. Cf. T. E. Lawrence's remark: 'So many plasticians [i.e. visual artists, especially sculptors] seem to admit to their notice the outside of machinery, and to exclude its purposefulness', *Letters of T. E. Lawrence*, David Garnett ed. (1938; my ref. to Spring Books, 1964 ed.), p. 591.

24. *Intro to New Existm*, pp. 15–16.

25. *Occult*, p. 41.

26. *Occult*, p. 763.

27. C. Wilson, *The Strength to Dream* (Gollancz, 1963; my refs. to Sphere Books, Abacus, 1976 ed.), pp. 191–92. Eliot quotation from *After Strange Gods* (1934).

28. Aldous Huxley, *Antic Hay* (1923; my ref. to Chatto & Windus, 1971 ed.), p. 47.

29. *Strength to Dream*, p. 221.

30. *Strength to Dream*, p. 174.

31. C. Wilson, *The Craft of the Novel* (Gollancz, 1975), p. 132.

32. *Strength to Dream*, p. 173.

33. 'Existential Criticism' in *Eagle and Earwig*, p. 64.

34. For Wilson's comments on H. G. Wells's later fiction, cf. Prefaces to *Man Without A Shadow* and *Philosopher's Stone*. In *Craft of the Novel*, however, Wilson seems to accept the conventional wisdom that after 1910, Wells 'began to go steadily downhill as a novelist' (p. 113). But this was not Wilson's view when he wrote most of the novels we are considering in this study. For his comments on David Lindsay, see 'Lindsay—*A Voyage to Arcturus*' in *Eagle and Earwig*, pp. 128–61, and C. Wilson, E. H. Visiak, J. B. Pick, *The Strange Genius of David Lindsay* (John Baker, 1970). For John Cowper Powys, see 'The Swamp and the Desert—Notes on Powys and Hemingway', *Eagle and Earwig*, pp. 113–27, 'Preface', *Man Without A Shadow*, and *Craft of the Novel*, pp. 163–65. For L. H. Myers, see 'L. H. Myers' in *Eagle and Earwig*, pp. 171–90, and *Craft of the Novel*, p. 150. For Bill Hopkins's *The Divine and the Decay*, see 'The Rope Trick—Bill Hopkins, Appendix II, *Beyond the Outsider*, pp. 207–25.

35. John A. Weigel in *Colin Wilson* (Boston, Twayne English Authors series No. 181, 1975) notes that 'every American campus has a group of enthusiastic supporters of Colin Wilson's ideas, youths who look upon him as a prophet', p. 139.

36. *Voyage*, pp. 160–61.

3

Novel Approaches

In his literary criticism, his remarks on literature in books on other subjects, and in the prefaces and postscripts to his fiction, Wilson has expressed strong and provocative views on the novel. No doubt these views, like those of every novelist on his craft are, to some extent, rationalizations of his own strengths and weaknesses; but they make up a consistent and challenging position. Although this position is given a distinctive character by Wilson's evolutionary existentialism, it is not without precedent. In particular, it is close to the position of the older H. G. Wells. We noted Wilson's admiration for Wells's later novels in the last chapter; in fact, Wilson has said that he suspects that Wells may be the greatest novelist of the twentieth century.[1] He asserts that Wells's now almost forgotten *World of William Clissold* (1926, 2 vols.) is as bold an experimental novel as *Ulysses* and, in its own way, as successful.[2] We shall look at the links between Wilson and Wells in this chapter. We shall also examine the relationship of Wilson's views on the novel to socialist ideas of literary commitment.

Like the later Wells, Wilson rejects both the novel which focuses on character, personal relationships, and local moral concerns, and the novel which is preoccupied with its own style and form. In Wells's time, these two modes of the novel tended to be fused together—as in the work of Henry James, with whom Wells had a celebrated dispute about the novel. In our time, there is often a gulf between the two modes (compare Margaret Drabble and Christine Brooke-Rose). Wilson argues, as Wells did, that both modes represent wrong directions for the novel: the novel should deal with ideas about the future possibilities of mankind.

Wilson shares with Wells a readiness to write his novels quickly and carelessly at times. This is partly due to economic pressures, and, in the 1960s, when most of Wilson's fiction was published, to his feeling of neglect. But it also springs from his belief that the primary importance of his novels is that they have something to say. He affirms: 'no amount of technique can ever form a substitute for the lack of having something to say.'[3] He would argue that to apply a 'close reading' technique to his novels, to point to stylistic lapses, and failures in characterization and dramaturgy, misses the point, which lies in the overall impact of the ideas. Wilson would endorse this claim by Wells:

> I had very many things to say, and . . . if I could say one of them in such a way as to get my point over to the reader, I did not worry much about finish.[4]

Wilson acknowledges, however, that 'finish' may contribute to 'getting one's point over'.

Wilson's emphasis on ideas, sometimes at the expense of style, characterization, and the immediacy of individual scenes, means that his novels, like Wells's, can be more interesting to think about than to read. The involvement in the reading process is lessened, at least on re-readings. This would not necessarily be wholly objectionable to Wilson, however. It could count as a kind of 'alienation effect', which directed the reader away from the performance of the text to its underlying ideas.

In his concern with ideas, Wilson is prepared to be unashamedly didactic. He would support Wells's belief in the need for 'a sort of argument with the reader, an explanation of the theory that is being exhibited'.[5] He feels himself to be, like Wells, and also like Bernard Shaw, a teacher, a prophet, with a vital message to convey. In most of his novels, however, he usually expresses his ideas, not through an authorial *persona*, but through a central character, who may also be a first-person narrator, holding ideas very close to his own.

Wilson argues that, even if the ideas in a novel become dated, the novel will still work as long as it communicates the energy of mind that animated those ideas. In his view, Wells's later novels survive, not because of the specific content of their ideas, but because of the enthusiasm with which Wells explored those ideas. Wilson's mentor, Bernard Shaw, makes a similar point about all art in his Preface to *Man and Superman*:

> Effectiveness of assertion is the Alpha and Omega of style. Disprove the assertion after it is made, yet its style remains. Darwin has no more destroyed the style of Job nor of Handel than Martin Luther destroyed the style of Giotto.[6]

Wilson believes that his assertions about man's evolutionary possibilities will be proved right, as Shaw believed that his assertions on the same matter would be; but the reader does not have to agree with these assertions to enjoy the work of either writer, though an important feature of their work is a constant demand for agreement.

Wilson is a kind of committed writer, though he describes his work as 'totally non-political'.[7] He has himself drawn an analogy between his attempt in his novels at what he calls an 'existential realism' and the socialist realism prescribed by Soviet ideology, as Wells drew analogies between his later fiction and the 'propaganda' novel.[8] He has praised Soviet literature for its active and optimistic premises and its seriousness.[9] He argues that both his approach and that of socialist realism reject a passive or pessimistic attitude to reality and aim to change things[10]; the same could be said of Wells. Wilson has affirmed that a question mark lies at the heart of most novels, but, like Wells and the socialist realists, he is concerned to find ways of effacing that question mark in his own fiction; he wants his novels to 'get somewhere'.[11] Wilson, however, would no doubt agree that Wells's point about the 'propaganda' novel is true of the socialist realist novel: both types of novel imply direction from outside. Wells felt that his novels were 'inner-directed'; Wilson would feel the same about his.

Wilson's 'inner-direction', like that of Wells, is provided by his desire for a positive future. Wilson has argued that the purpose of the novel is to create a self-image for its author— not merely in the sense of an autobiographical self-projection, although the heroes of his novels are usually self-projections, but in the sense of an image of what the author wants.[12] Wilson wants to further the evolutionary development of mankind; his novels are self-images in the sense that they are projections of that desire; they explore the imperatives and possibilities of a positive future.

The central feature that Wilson has in common with both Wells and the socialist realists is a belief in a positive future. He has endorsed the idea that all novels are 'thought experiments' and in his own fiction he experiments with his ideas of the potentialities of man.[13] Like all his work, his novels are an attempt at a re-definition of man in the light of the future.

In contrast to Wells and the socialist realists, however, Wilson does not believe in the primary importance to man's future of social and political matters and he hardly touches on them in his novels. Although he has argued that the purpose of the novels is to achieve what he calls 'wide-angle consciousness', a 'bird's-eye view' of existence that takes in as much as possible, his field of vision is, in a sense, exceptionally narrow.[14] He concentrates on what he sees as the essential question: the meaning and purpose of human existence: a question that cannot, he believes, be answered adequately on the social and political plane, or in terms of human relationships. It is this approach which makes him claim kinship with the tradition of the European rather than the English novel, insofar as the former is concerned with man's relationship to God or to his absence as well as, or instead of, his relationship to other people and to social and political matters. Wilson's solution to the problem of man's need for God, his way of attempting to efface the question mark in his novels, is not a return to traditional religion, or a stoical or despairing acceptance of God's absence, but, of course, his evolutionary existentialism. Wilson believes that his evolutionary perspective in fact produces a heightened form of 'wide-angle consciousness' in his novels, a 'bird's-eye view' that rises above ordinary human concerns, that is akin to the long-term view a god might have.

Wilson believes in putting his ideas into his novels, but recognizes that, as well as direct statements of those ideas, put into the mouths or minds of his characters, the novel as a whole can make an indirect statement of them, and one, moreover, which functions on more levels than does straightforward

43

exposition. It is primarily in this sense that he sees his novels as 'a manner of philosophizing'. Thus, despite his kinship with Wells and his lapses of style and dramaturgy, he is far more concerned than was Wells in his later fiction to give his novels form and make them accessible to a wide readership. His novels draw their forms from two main sources: the *Bildungsroman*, the kind of novel, most common in German literature, which deals with the personal development of a single individual, and popular fiction of the kind that played an important role in his early life. When he was working on the early versions of *Ritual in the Dark*, he also had an interest in the 'mythic method'—T. S. Eliot's term for Joyce's use of the *Odyssey* to structure a novel about the modern world. As we saw in Chapter One, Wilson intended at one time to base the structure of *Ritual* upon the *Egyptian Book of the Dead*. He later dropped this idea; but his novels can still be seen as employing a kind of mythic method, through their use of popular forms. We shall consider this shortly.

In *The Outsider*, Wilson offers some definitions of the *Bildungsroman* which apply to his own use of the genre:

> The *Bildungsroman* . . . is fictional biography that is mainly concerned with its hero's reaction to ideas, or the development of his ideas about 'life' from his experience. [It] is a sort of laboratory in which the hero conducts an experiment in living. For this reason, it is a particularly useful medium for writers whose main concern is a philosophical answer to that practical question: What shall we do with our lives? . . . The *Bildungsroman* is the natural form of serious fictional art, no matter how short the period of the hero's life that it treats.[15]

As we shall see, most of Wilson's novels, especially the earlier ones, are in some measure *Bildungsroman* which show the existential and, later, the evolutionary development of the hero, with the help of one or two other characters, usually 'larger-than-life' figures who act as unofficial 'teachers'. In his later novels, however, the popular form technique becomes more prominent than the use of the form of the *Bildungsroman*. Even his first four novels use structures and elements from popular forms, and from *Necessary Doubt* onwards, the popular form becomes the dominant one; he draws upon the detective story, science fiction, the 'true crime' story, the pornographic novel and the spy story.

Wilson's use of popular forms has a number of functions. It gives an overall structure to his novels which prevents them from becoming, as some of Wells's later novels did, purely expository; it acts, as Wilson puts it, as 'a kind of carnival mask' behind which he can explore his ideas.[16] It symbolizes, especially in his later work, the non-empirical order of reality, the web of meaning which, Wilson has increasingly come to believe, underlies the apparent contingency of the everyday world. It further symbolizes the serious concerns of his novels— for example, in *The Black Room*, the quest for a way to resist the black room, ostensibly in the interests of espionage, symbolizes the evolutionary quest. As there is, however, always an ironic divergence between the aims implied by the popular form— those of solving a murder mystery in *The Glass Cage*, for instance—and the aims of the evolutionary existentialist, who is usually the central character, the relationship between popular form and serious significance is one of both difference and symbolic analogy: an interesting tension is set up. In using popular forms in this structuring and symbolic way, Wilson is, in a sense, practising the 'mythic method', insofar as popular forms can be seen as debased myths.

The use of popular forms also enables Wilson to reach a wider audience, at least on some level, than he would otherwise be likely to command. He wants to do this not simply for financial reasons, although these naturally play their part: he is primarily motivated by his Wellsian-Shavian desire to educate and communicate. He also, as we saw in the last chapter, dislikes the gap which has opened up between serious and popular literature in the twentieth century. Moreover, as pointed out in Chapter One, his exposure to popular literature as a child had taught him how such literature could both stimulate the imagination and represent more serious concerns. From an early age, the serious and the popular co-existed in his mind, and it is this co-existence that the popular forms and elements in his novels reflect.

Wilson has claimed that his use of popular forms aims to 'bring Brecht's alienation effect to the novel by aiming at an effect approximating to parody'.[17] This idea of parodying popular forms to achieve *Verfremdung* is a good one, and we should bear it in mind as we consider Wilson's novels in detail, but he does not put it into practice very successfully. Parody demands a rigorous, sophisticated balance between involvement in the style and attitudes its author is mocking and detachment from them; Wilson tends to become too involved with his popular forms to achieve successful parody all that often; perhaps this is why he speaks ambiguously of 'an effect approximating to parody'. It may be that, in view of his early reading, the popular and serious are insufficiently distinct in his own mind. Furthermore, although Wilson can achieve humour in his novels, his general earnestness is alien to the lightheartedness that parody, even if it is directed towards a serious end, requires. He does, however, achieve an alienation effect, partly by the stylistic and dramatic lapses which we spoke of earlier and, more importantly and deliberately, by means of the divergence between the evolutionary existentialist concerns of the novel, usually focused in the hero, and the concerns implied by the popular form.

Let us sum up, then, how we should approach Wilson's novels, on the basis of the attitudes outlined in this chapter. We should not expect to find a concern with character, personal relationships, or social and political man; we should not be disappointed if we do not find a prose that is continuously vivid, original and precise; we should not look for a self-reflexive concern with the form and practice of the novel; we should not expect sustained parody. If we want these things, we must look elsewhere. We can hope to find, however, an obsessive concern with the problem of meaning and purpose in human existence; an exploration of the solution to this problem that, in Wilson's view, evolutionary existentialism can provide; a readiness to express ideas both directly, through characters, and indirectly, through the structure and events of the novel; a prose that does have the quality of 'effectiveness of assertion'; a strong element of the *Bildungsroman*, with the hero undergoing an education and sometimes an initiation at the hands of life, usually helped by unofficial 'teachers'; elements and structures of popular forms, with the popular form, from *Necessary Doubt* onwards, becoming the chief structuring device; a divergence between the concerns implied by the popular forms and elements and the concerns of evolutionary existentialism; and, above all, a positive orientation to the future. With all these points in mind, we shall now turn to our detailed examination of Wilson's novels.

NOTES

1. 'Prefatory Note', *Philosopher's Stone*, p. 5. But cf. n. 34, Chapter Two.
2. 'Preface', *Man Without A Shadow*, p. 12.
3. *Strength to Dream*, p. 79.
4. *Expt in Autobiography*, II, p. 497. The whole 'Digression about Novels', pp. 487–504 is well worth reading both in itself, and with relevance to Wilson's approach to the novel.
5. *Expt in Autobiography*, II, p. 498.
6. Bernard Shaw, 'Epistle Dedicatory' to *Man and Superman* (Constable, 1903), xxxv.
7. Entry under 'Wilson, Colin' in J. Vinson ed., *Contemporary Novelists* (St. James's Press, 2nd ed., 1976), p. 1521.
8. 'Preface', *Man Without A Shadow*, p. 14. *Expt in Autobiography*, II, p. 496.
9. C. Wilson, 'Culture in the Soviet Union', Appendix III *Beyond the Outsider*, pp. 219–25.
10. 'Preface', *Man Without A Shadow*, p. 14.
11. *Craft of the Novel*, p. 20.
12. *Craft of the Novel*, pp. 21–30.
13. *Craft of the Novel*, pp. 69–70.
14. *Craft of the Novel*, pp. 82–7.
15. *Outsider*, pp. 61–2.
16. *Contemporary Novelists*, p. 1521.
17. 'Note', *God of the Labyrinth*, p. 283.

4

Metaphysical Thriller:
Ritual in the Dark

Ritual in the Dark, Wilson's first novel, is a powerful metaphysical thriller. It combines a number of modes: the realistic novel of the 1950s; the *Bildungsroman*; the murder story. It also contains elements of fantasy and myth. All these fuse into a rich totality. In Chapter Three, it was stated that Wilson's novels could be more interesting to think about than to read: this is not true of *Ritual*. It is fascinating to think about; but it is no less fascinating to read and re-read.

Insofar as it is a realistic novel, *Ritual* renders, with careful naturalistic detail, the London of the 1950s that Wilson knew as a young man. We walk along its streets and across its bomb-sites; we enter run-down lodgings, a house in Hampstead, a Catholic hostel, a block of luxury flats, a Soho café, and a homosexual club and brothel. This realism provides a solid basis for the metaphysical explorations of the novel.

As a *Bildungsroman*, *Ritual* gives an account of the rapid development of a young man of 26, Gerard Sorme. Most of the heroes of Wilson's novels will be, in essential respects, self-portraits or self-projections, and Sorme is the closest to his author. He has the typical characteristics of the Wilson hero. He is deeply concerned for spiritual development; he is inwardly detached from external events; he lives more by thought than by instinct and emotion. But he also has a relish for food, drink and sex.

Sorme, however, gets more fully involved with people than

the heroes of some of Wilson's later novels, and this helps to enrich the human dimension of *Ritual*. Together with the realistic detail, this dimension relates *Ritual* to the traditional English novel, which focuses on human relationships in a more-or-less realistic setting.

We learn that Sorme, before the action of the novel begins, is supposed to have spent five years in isolation, supported by a small private income, trying to develop himself spiritually. While we are not quite convinced that the Sorme we meet in the novel is likely to have spent so long alone in 'celibacy, partial boredom, the unsuccessful attempt to harvest his own solitude'[1]—the idea of Sorme as celibate particularly strains our credulity—the symbolic point stands. Isolation has not brought enlightenment; for Sorme, as for Zarathustra, there must be a down-going.

Sorme's has been a life where things do not happen; but from the moment he meets Austin Nunne, things start to happen at a rapid pace; indeed, Sorme's *Bildung* is compressed into a remarkably short time. Through Nunne, he meets the demure spinster Gertrude Quincey, who is Nunne's aunt, and her pretty 16-year-old niece, Caroline; be begins affairs with both of them. He also meets Oliver Glasp, a self-tormenting painter, and Father Carruthers, an invalid Catholic priest. Independently of Nunne, he finds out about a series of Jack the Ripper-style murders in Whitechapel, and he becomes fascinated by them. Through all these experiences, Sorme gains insight into himself and his own possibilities; the upward trajectory of his development gives *Ritual* an optimistic atmosphere, a sense of light and space, that transcends the unpleasantness of some of its themes—especially the theme of murder.

In the first half of *Ritual*, we find that Sorme is prone to violent, misanthropic feelings, and sometimes has glimpses into the metaphysical abyss:

> That night, the vastation happened again. He woke up feeling hot and slightly drunk. He was still fully clothed, lying on the bed. Opposite his eyes, the radio droned softly; he had fallen asleep listening to a late night chamber concert. The room was in darkness, except for the light from the wave-length panel, and the red glow of the neon lights from the cinema over the way. His mind formed the question as he stared across the room: What am

I doing here? It seemed arbitrary; he might have been anywhere or anything. A sense of alien-ness oppressed him, and he tried to focus his attention on it to discover its precise nature. Immediately, an orgasm of fear twisted his heart, and drained the strength out of his will. It was an awareness that his own existence was not capable of detaching itself from existence to question it. Existence faced him like a blank wall. There was an instinctive desire to penetrate the wall, to assert his reality beyond it, and a terror that came with the recognition that he was trapped in existence, that no detachment from it was possible. The terror was like losing an arm: too violent to hurt.[2]

As his life opens up, however, he develops a stronger sense of meaning and purpose. At times, this reaches a peak of affirmation and clarity: for example, one night when, after talking to Nunne, he climbs on to the roof of his boarding-house:

The parapet was a foot high; it enclosed two sides of the roof, facing north and east. On the west side, only a gutter divided the slates from the drop past five stories to the waste ground between the house and the church. The breeze was cold. He moved round the angle of the roof to shelter from it, then sat cautiously on the slates, his feet braced against the parapet. Towards Camden Town, the lights of the plastics factory that worked all night lit the sky. The exhilaration was still in him, relaxing into a sense of quiet and power. When the sound of a heavy lorry passed on the Kentish Town Road his mind moved ahead of it, through Whetstone and Barnet, to the north. The thoughts were controlled, clear-cut and deliberate. The feeling that drove them seemed to flow steadily and certainly. They moved towards an image of gratitude, of reverence, of affirmation; it became a cathedral, bigger than any known cathedral, symbol of the unseen. He thought: This has taken me five years. A vision of all knowledge, of human achievement in imagination and courage. Not the mystic's vision, but the philosopher's, freed from triviality and immediacy. I am the god who dwelleth in the eye, and I have come to give right and truth to Ra.[3]

In both the above passages, we can see how Wilson's careful rendering of naturalistic detail helps to ground Sorme's metaphysical experiences, to make them more convincing. We will also observe how Wilson conveys the analytic quality of Sorme's consciousness: Sorme is not content merely to experience extremes of terror and vision: he wants to understand and explain them. In this, he embodies Wilson's own belief in the importance of analysis as an antidote to Romantic confusion and despair.

Ritual in the Dark could be seen as the story of Sorme's encounter with the temptations and possibilities of Romanticism; the whole novel could be read as a sustained critique of Romanticism. This critique is dramatized most fully in the relationship between Sorme and Austin Nunne. Nunne is the first of those larger-than-life characters often found in Wilson's novels. He is rich, hedonistic, homosexual; an aesthete who writes on ballet; a physically powerful man with sadistic tendencies. To Sorme, he is a Mephistopheles and an enigma; a magic mirror in which Sorme can see a negative self-image; a dark *Doppelganger* who deepens Sorme's sense of purpose; a teacher who instructs by his own black example. Above all, in the first half of the novel, he is a reincarnation of Nijinsky.

The link between Nunne and Nijinsky is established at the outset of the novel, when Sorme meets Nunne at an exhibition about the Russian ballet impresario, Diaghilev, and registers Nunne's likeness to Nijinsky. Wilson evocatively re-creates the Diaghilev exhibition designed by Richard Buckle, which actually took place in London in 1953. In the novel, the exhibition symbolizes the kind of Romanticism which draws Sorme to Nunne. Through mimetic visual display (such as the mock-up of a Paris street scene), music (Stravinsky and Prokofiev), and the odour of Diaghilev's favourite scent, Mitsouko, the exhibition makes a rich synaesthetic appeal. It stimulates the sense of other times and places, of fuller dimensions of being, that Wilson ascribes, in *The Occult*, to 'Faculty X'. At the same time, there is something suspect about this stimulation: it is too sensual, too heady, too thoughtless.

Nunne arouses 'feelings of attraction and repulsion' in Sorme;[4] but once Sorme has established that he is not homosexual, their friendship develops quickly. Soon, he gains a remarkable insight into Nunne's psyche. To his surprise, Nunne rings him from Switzerland and asks him to visit a basement flat he owns in London. He is to collect some women's clothes that Nunne has left there and return to their shelves any books lying around. It later turns out that this is

51

Nunne's way of testing Sorme, of seeing if he can trust him; it is also, we suspect, Nunne's attempt to establish a greater intimacy with Sorme: an indirect confession about his secret life.

The flat reveals the dark side of the kind of Romanticism symbolized by the Diaghilev exhibition. The analogy with the exhibition is immediately suggested when Sorme enters the flat to find a strong smell of Mitsouko, and it is developed when he penetrates into an inner room which is like a model of Nunne's mind. There, in Nunne's absence, Sorme comes much closer to him; it is not surprising that at one point he finds a 'curious sense of Nunne's presence . . . beginning to grow in him'.[5]

The room resembles a set for an Expressionist drama. The walls are almost covered by black velvet curtains, the carpet and divan are wine-red, the ceiling night-blue. Lighting is provided by blue bulbs, as in the display of a haunted theatre which Sorme and Nunne saw at the Diaghilev exhibition; it was in that exhibit that the smell of Mitsouko was strongest. The room arouses in Sorme the same response that Nunne aroused at the exhibition: attraction and repulsion.

This time, however, repulsion comes to the fore: we meet Romanticism gone rotten. Sorme finds obscene drawings, an edition of de Sade, and medical textbooks on sexual deviance. As Nunne requested, he looks for any books lying around; he finds one called *Criminology, Its Background and Techniques*:

> He turned it over, and found himself looking at a photograph of a woman with her throat cut.[6]

At first he feels sick and goes out of the room. Recovering, he forces himself to return and look through the book, and then at other books on forensic medicine that are on Nunne's shelves. This provokes an experience he has had before: the vastation.

This time, however, the vastation is objectified in the images of violent death the books contain. The vastation cannot be reduced to the apprehension of violent death, but violent death is the 'objective correlative' in *Ritual in the Dark* to the metaphysical nihilism of the vastation. Sorme will see this himself as the novel draws to a close.

From Nunne's flat, Sorme goes to see Father Carruthers, whom he has already got to know. Carruthers confirms that Nunne has sadistic tendencies; Sorme expresses his fears that the police may suspect that Nunne has some connection with the Whitechapel murders. Suspicion may be starting to grow in Sorme himself; but his fascination with Nunne has yet to reach its climax.

This occurs when Nunne takes him to a homosexual club and brothel—Sorme is, of course, an interested observer rather than a potential client. Already bloated with food and drink, Sorme drinks more, and is violently sick; Nunne finds him a single bedroom on an upper floor of the brothel. As day dawns, Sorme has a dream, echoing the ballet *Le Spectre de la Rose*, in which Nunne's apotheosis occurs.

> Nunne was standing by the window, staring out. In the faint dawnlight, the big naked body looked like a marble statue. The shoulders were broad; rounded muscle, a dancer's shoulders.
>
> Sorme could not see his eyes. They would be stone eyes, not closed, immobile in the half light, nor like the eyes of the priest, grey in the ugly gargoyle's face. When he closed his own eyes, he saw the dancer, the big body, moving without effort through the air, slowly, unresisted, then coming to earth, as silent as a shadow. It was very clear. The face, slim and muscular, bending over him, a chaplet of rose leaves woven into the hair, a faun's face, the brown animal eyes smiling at him, beyond good and evil.
>
> . . . .
>
> And then the leap, violent as the sun on ice, beyond the bed, floating without noise, on, through the open window.
>
> The excitement rose in him like a fire. The rose, bloodblack in the silver light, now reddening in the dawn that blows over Paddington's roof-tops. Ending. A rose thrown from an open window, curving high over London's waking roof-tops, then falling, its petals loosening, into the grey soiled waters of the Thames.
>
> He wanted to say it, with the full shock of amazement: So that's who you are.
>
> Certain now, as never before, the identification complete.
>
> It was still there as he woke up, the joy and surprise of the discovery, fading as he looked around the lightening room. He said aloud: Vaslav.[7]

53

We need to compare this with Sorme's vision on the roof of his boarding-house. That was a highly conscious one: the vision of the philosopher. By contrast, Nunne's apotheosis occurs in the regions of dream and hallucination; it appeals to the emotions, it carries us away; it is very much a Romantic experience, like those Sorme had at the Diaghilev exhibition and in Nunne's flat. It is both intoxicating and destructive: Vaslav-Nunne the Romantic, exalted in a dream, is doomed to fall, whereas Sorme, on the roof-top, experienced his exaltation in the real world, and climbed cautiously down from the heights to continue the quest. Nunne's apotheosis, which closes the first half of *Ritual in the Dark*, is also the beginning of his downfall: it is the zenith of Sorme's fascination with him, and of his identification of Nunne with Nijinsky. Vaslav's dying fall into the Thames anticipates Nunne's accelerating pace of self-destruction, and his decline in the eyes of Sorme.

In the second half of the novel, Sorme's suspicion that Nunne may be the Whitechapel killer strengthens as the murder hunt closes in. Though he continues to think and talk about Nunne, he becomes increasingly detached from him. He meets him in person again on only two occasions. The first time, Nunne introduces him to two American 'Beat' poets, the 'Chicago Rebels'. Sorme's encounter with them contributes further to the novel's critique of Romanticism. With their passion for jazz, drink, drugs and wild living, the poets are modern incarnations of the Romantic spirit. Significantly, *Ritual in the Dark* was first published in 1960, at the start of the decade when this form of Romanticism was to achieve widespread popularity among young people in the West, and was to become associated, in some of its manifestations, with violence.

Though unimpressed by the Chicago Rebels, Sorme still experiences the fascination of Nunne:

> the brown eyes were as soft as an animal's and as sardonic and caressing as a heathen god. For a moment Sorme felt again the curious awe and submission that he had felt before in Nunne's presence; the sense of being with someone of a different species.[8]

The meeting gives them little opportunity to talk intimately with each other, however. That opportunity comes in Sorme's final meeting with Nunne, near the end of the novel. The police are on their way to take Nunne in for questioning; Sorme gets there before them, to warn him. In a powerful and moving scene, Nunne confirms that he is the Whitechapel killer, but Sorme still cannot bring himself to wholly condemn him: his ambivalence in this respect, which gives *Ritual in the Dark* much of its disturbing power, is dramatized most strongly here.

As Sorme and Nunne prepare to leave, the police arrive and take Nunne in for questioning. Sorme realizes, however, that they have no real evidence. He returns to London and goes to see Father Carruthers once more. He tells him that he now knows Nunne is the murderer. While they are talking, Stein arrives. Stein, a friend of Carruthers, is a psychiatrist and pathologist working with the police on the murders. He suspects that Sorme knows Nunne to be guilty, and hopes to persuade him to give evidence to the police. He takes Sorme to a mortuary to see the corpse of Nunne's latest victim.

Sorme is not affected as Stein hopes; there seems to be no link between the corpse and a live human being. Then, to relieve the pressure Stein is applying, he asks to see a corpse that lies under another sheet; it is a woman who was killed when her husband threw a paraffin lamp at her. While Stein leaves him for a moment, Sorme contemplates it:

> The sight of the corpse produced no revulsion or horror; only a recognition of humanity. He pulled back the sheet from the whole body, and stared at it. It was too obviously and recognisably the body of the young woman. Where the charred flesh came to an end, the skin was burnt and raw. Fragments of clothing still adhered to her legs and arms. The fascination was one of pity and kinship. . . . The flesh had once been caressed; the body had carried children. He felt the stirring of a consuming curiosity about her. Why was she dead? Who was she? There was an absurdity in her death. How could twenty-five years as a human being lead inevitably to a mortuary slab, the breasts and smooth belly carbonised out of relevance to life? The belly and thighs were well-shaped. If she had been alive, sleeping, he would have felt the movement of desire: its failure symbolised the absurdity of her death.[9]

It is these reflections which provoke Sorme's final rejection of Nunne. He realizes that violent death is the 'objective correlative', the realization in physical terms, of the metaphysical vastation. His conversion happens quickly; but he has been building towards it, without quite knowing it, for a long time. His affirmative development was bound, in the end, to make him reject Nunne, as his own ultimate negation, a walking vastation, who has lived out the nihilistic rather than the puritanical connotations of his surname.

Wilson's critique of Romanticism in *Ritual in the Dark* is also dramatized through Sorme's relationship with Oliver Glasp. In contrast to Nunne, Glasp is genuinely creative, a brilliant painter; like Nunne, he is obsessed with pain and suffering, but in a self-tormenting rather than sadistic way. To some extent, he is based on Wilson's idea of Van Gogh. Despite Glasp's misanthropy, Sorme soon strikes up a friendship with him, and they talk about art, about sex, about suffering, and about murder. Sorme comes to feel, however, that Glasp, like Nunne, is a victim of Romanticism: if Nunne is too susceptible to his sensual impulses, Glasp is too susceptible to his emotions. Glasp has an intense but non-sexual relationship with a 12-year-old girl; she comes from a slum background, but she is sensitive and artistically talented. Her father brings an unwarranted charge of seducing a minor against Glasp; a medical examination reveals that the girl is not a virgin, but she admits that her cousin was responsible. The charge is dropped, but Glasp is shattered at the disclosure of the girl's 'impurity'. To Sorme, his reaction is the clinching evidence of his limitations:

> He's too emotional . . . He's a typical romantic. I've come to the conclusion that the twentieth century's suffering from a romantic hangover.[10]

Despite Glasp's emotional Romanticism, he functions in the novel as a corrective to the decadent sensual Romanticism of Nunne. Glasp challenges Sorme's fascination with Nunne:

> something goes wrong with a man who wastes time. He starts to go rotten. You can almost smell him. Don't you feel that about Austin?[11]

Sorme dissents from this view at the time; but at the end of the novel, he denounces Nunne to Gertrude Quincey in these words:

> there's a part of [Austin's] brain that's as rotten as a rotten apple. He's let it get that way. He's let himself go rotten.[12]

The echo of Glasp is clear.

As well as being a realistic novel, a *Bildungsroman*, and a critique of Romanticism, *Ritual in the Dark* is also a murder thriller. This aspect of the novel anticipates Wilson's use of popular forms in his later fiction. Though the thriller plot has a less dominant role in *Ritual* than in a later novel such as *The Glass Cage*, it performs similar structural and symbolic functions: it gives the novel form and direction, and symbolizes the dark, uncertain side of existence: the abyss apprehended by Sorme in his vastations. The thriller plot also enables Wilson to develop the novel as a critique of Romanticism by exploring Sorme's Romantic fascination with murder.

Sorme feels that his misanthropic, violent moments, his aversion to everyday life, his desire for intensity, all enable him, to some extent, to understand and identify with the murderer, even before he suspects that it may be Nunne. He tells Glasp: 'I can see certain aspects of myself reflected in the murderer.'[13] In this respect, it is interesting to note that, in earlier versions of *Ritual*, the hero was the murderer.[14] As the novel proceeds, Sorme comes closer and closer to the reality of murder. He sees the photographs of murder victims in Nunne's books; he goes with a reporter friend to the scene of one murder, on a night when the killer has struck twice; Stein takes him to see the corpse of the latest victim. He also becomes increasingly aware that Nunne may be the murderer. As we have seen, however, it is not until he sees the corpse of the burned woman, whom Nunne did not kill, that the reality of violent death comes home to him: the spell of murder is broken: Sorme is at last free. The exploration of Sorme's ambivalent response to murder is a fascinating and disturbing aspect of *Ritual in the Dark*.

Sartre has said that 'the law is theatre', that the stage is a courtroom in which a case is tried.[15] This can also apply to novels, and *Ritual in the Dark* can be seen as a murder trial. Like any murder trial, it involves some of the deepest human feelings. Sorme acts as defending counsel, but he is no detached professional; he is strongly identified with his client, even when he is anonymous, and his growing suspicion that Nunne may be the murderer gives his defence immediate concrete implications. To defend the murderer is to defend Nunne, and Sorme does so under greater and greater pressure—to Father Carruthers, to Glasp, to Gertrude Quincey, to Stein. He affirms time and again that Nunne, killer though he may be, is not insane. In the end, however, he recants and turns prosecuting counsel. He tells Gertrude Quincey: '[Austin's] insane . . . I wanted to understand him, not condemn him. . . . If I saw him now, I'd have to make him realize that I condemn him.' He does not denounce Nunne to the police, however; Gertrude Quincey goes to visit Nunne's wealthy parents to persuade them to have their son confined in a private mental home. Sorme feels that Nunne is finished anyway: 'He might as well be dead.'[16]

Woven in with the murder story in *Ritual in the Dark* is an exploration of sexuality. Nunne's vicious, decadent sexuality, which leads him to murder, contrasts with the vigorous hetero-sexuality of Sorme, but there are similarities as well as differences. The humorous and tender aspects of Sorme's relation-ships with Gertrude Quincey and Caroline, effectively evoked by Wilson, are, we feel, beyond Nunne; but Sorme's inability to choose between the two women, which continues throughout the novel, reveals his self-division, the amoral imperatives of his sexual impulse: there is an analogy with Nunne here. Caroline, with her frank, innocent, slightly coarse sexuality, stands, like Nunne, for sensuous, physical life—and Sorme finds 'a futility inherent in physical life that frightened him'.[17] When Sorme takes Caroline's virginity, he inadvertently hurts her at first: pain can be a part of 'normal' sexuality too. In the end, however, Caroline transcends pain and enjoys the experience: pain is not, as it is for Nunne, involved in the ultimate excite-ment. The contrasts and comparisons between conventional and deviant sexuality add to the complexity of the novel.

Ritual in the Dark is a rich, multi-faceted fiction. In this chapter, it has been possible to point out only its major facets: there are many other intriguing areas to be explored. For example, the significance of Nijinsky in the novel could be probed more deeply, bringing in Nijinsky's diary, and Wilson's discussion of him in *The Outsider*; the resemblance of Glasp to

Van Gogh could be considered further, again with reference to *The Outsider* and to Van Gogh's *Letters*; the Egyptian symbolism could be examined, in the light of Wilson's original intention to base the structure of *Ritual* on the *Egyptian Book of the Dead*. There are many possibilities.

In his later fiction, Wilson will develop some of the features of *Ritual in the Dark* and discard others. His concern with the quest for intenser consciousness, with sexuality, and with murder will, of course, persist. His use of the thriller as a structural and symbolic device will become the basis of his popular form technique. On the other hand, those features which link *Ritual* most closely to the traditional novel—the evocation of human character and human relationships in a carefully rendered naturalistic setting—will fade in importance. We can see this happening in his next three novels.

NOTES

1. *Ritual in the Dark* (Gollancz, 1960), p. 191.
2. *Ritual*, p. 41.
3. *Ritual*, pp. 137–38.
4. *Ritual*, p. 11.
5. *Ritual*, p. 107.
6. *Ritual*, p. 108.
7. *Ritual*, pp. 179–80.
8. *Ritual*, pp. 248–49.
9. *Ritual*, p. 398.
10. *Ritual*, p. 357.
11. *Ritual*, pp. 283–84.
12. *Ritual*, p. 410.
13. *Ritual*, p. 206.
14. *World of Colin Wilson*, pp. 178–86.
15. Jean-Paul Sartre, 'Interview with Kenneth Tynan (1961)' in Michel Contat and Michel Rybalka ed., *Sartre on Theater* [*sic*], trans. by Frank Jellinek (Quartet Books, 1976), pp. 126–27.
16. *Ritual*, pp. 409–10, 412.
17. *Ritual*, p. 125.

5

Novels of Transition: *Adrift in Soho*, *The World of Violence*, *Man Without A Shadow*

Ritual in the Dark, in its numerous versions, had preoccupied Wilson for many years. Now that it had been published at last, the question for him as a novelist was: Where next? Another *Ritual*—an exploration of existential extremes within the conventions of a realistic novel—or a new departure? His next three works of fiction are more preparations for a new departure than that departure itself; they are novels of transition, which show Wilson searching for a method.

His second novel, *Adrift in Soho* (1961), is much more light-hearted than *Ritual*. Like *Ritual*, it is a *Bildungsroman* and an exploration of the modes of freedom; but if *Ritual* is a metaphysical thriller, *Adrift* is a metaphysical comedy.

Harry Preston, a young, unknown writer, is discharged from National Service in the R.A.F. due to 'nervous unsuitability'. He is given two months' discharge pay. After a few rather aimless weeks in his home town in the Midlands, he sets out for London. As with Sorme at the Diaghilev exhibition, things start to happen to Harry from the moment he arrives in the capital. In a Soho pub, he meets James, a charming con-man, and Doreen, an attractive young New Zealand girl. Thrown out of his lodgings after letting James spend the night there with a girl,

Harry agrees with James to form a 'league for mutual support'. James shows him how to survive with no fixed abode or income, but Harry soon finds this tiring and demoralizing. Doreen puts him up for the night, along with two more of her acquaintances, but she is then evicted from her lodgings. Harry takes her to a house in Notting Hill, to which James introduced him, where a variety of drifters and aspiring artists live. On the top floor lives Ricky Prelati, an unknown painter of genius. Harry and Doreen move into a room there. James brings Sir Reginald Propter, a wealthy patron of the arts, to see Ricky's paintings; impressed, Propter goes on television to publicize them, without telling Ricky, who so far has avoided exhibiting his work. Ricky suddenly finds himself famous. He decides to barricade himself in his room to get on with his painting; but a girl arrives whom he had earlier agreed to take as a model. The novel ends there; it seems that it will now be difficult for Ricky to find privacy.

Above all, *Adrift in Soho* is a *Bildungsroman*, a novel of a young man's education in and by the world. Harry could be a younger version of Sorme; indeed, *Adrift* is much more like a first novel than *Ritual* in some ways. Like Sorme, Harry is open to experience in the outer world of people and events, but he is inwardly detached; he longs for solitude and the chance to think, write and meditate, but he doubts if he can sustain a sense of purpose in isolation. Wilson has said that *Adrift* uses the form of the picaresque novel, and there is some truth in this;[1] but Harry is not the traditional *picaro*, a mere name on which to hang events. He has a character, a weight of his own which, so to speak, pulls against events. Like Sorme, Harry constantly analyses his experiences and, as *Adrift* is a first-person narrative, his analyses often come across in a more direct and didactic way than Sorme's; even more evidently than Sorme, Harry is a moralist, who is sympathetic to others but tends to judge and categorize them.

This didactic element does not take over the novel, however; it is balanced by the economical, effective, and often very funny rendering of people, places, and events. The London of the 1950s, which Wilson knew as a young man, comes to life: a London of lodging-houses, cheap cafés, secondhand bookshops, pubs, impossible landladies, con-men, bohemians, drifters, neurotics, tramps, eccentrics, would-be and genuine

61

artists. All these features could be found in present-day London, of course; but the atmosphere is quite different. *Adrift* is a documentary which captures a period that is close to us in time, but distant from us in flavour.

Despite this documentary aspect, *Adrift* is not a wholly realistic novel. It takes us up and carries us along effortlessly; we at once suspend disbelief; and the narrative skill and naturalistic detail may prevent us from realizing that we are reading a kind of fairytale. A young man goes to London, at once meets lots of interesting people, has many vivid experiences, finds an attractive girl, gets a room in the same house as a painter of genius who suddenly becomes famous, and is offered a congenial job as a publisher's reader by Sir Reginald Propter. The ease with which Harry conquers London, like a bohemian Dick Whittington, is one of *Adrift*'s delightful qualities. Once we recognize it, we also recognize its two functions: to expose the novel as fiction, and symbolize an order beneath the apparent contingency of the everyday world.

The 'Introductory' section of *Adrift* is an important prelude to the main action. It could stand alone as a short story. It conveys very well the atmosphere of provincial futility into which Harry enters after leaving the R.A.F. The discharge pay means that he need not work for a time, and he determines to write every day in the reference library; he finds that he cannot. He takes a job as a labourer on a building site and settles into an automatic routine in a 'world without values'.

Then his grandfather dies.

> I was not upset by his death because I did not believe in it. Death was illogical. Either he was not dead, or he had never been alive. But the world was still the same; everything went on. You could not convince me that something had *happened*. I sat there and thought: That's it. *Things don't happen.* If they happened, the world would need a complete reassessment. But as human beings we proceed on the assumption that things won't happen. That was why I might have stayed in the navvying job for twenty years and become a foreman; that was why people got up every morning and went off to work and married a girl who seemed attractive and made the best of her for the rest of their lives. The world slides on, easily and silently; there is nothing to get excited about because there is nothing to be gained and nothing lost.

Whatever is real has nothing to do with this world where things don't happen. And nothing matters.[2]

This perception of automacy frees him from it. The next day, he sets off for London.

Once he gets to London, his education proceeds apace; he comes under the tutelage of two masters. The first is James. James is not merely a charming but unscrupulous con-man. He has altruistic moments—for example, he shows Propter Ricky Prelati's work, from apparently disinterested motives— and he has, as Harry eventually comes to realize, a sincere 'philosophy of freedom' that is 'really a kind of vision, and not just an excuse for doing nothing'.[3] He is, in fact, a prophet who wants disciples and sees Harry as a likely candidate. At one point Harry describes his relationship with James as that of 'the sorcerer's apprentice'.[4]

For James, however, freedom is horizontal, on one plane; freedom from work, mortgage, respectability. He enlists Harry's sympathy, but Harry has glimpses of a greater, vertical freedom. These glimpses, like Sorme's in *Ritual*, are 'spots of time' that slow down the narrative pace—hectic in this novel— and open a gap between the external events of the story and Harry's inner development. Here is a notable example:

> As I walked down the Tottenham Court Road ... I was suddenly overwhelmed by a kind of brainstorm of insight. These experiences have happened to me at regular periods throughout my life; they are a sudden act of adjustment, a revolt against the world I have been persuaded by its immediacy to accept. ...
>
> I ... stopped by the lighted window of a bookshop, and stood looking at expensive volumes on art. The centre of the window was occupied by a display, designed to sell some new set of art books. An automatic device turned over pages set in a metal frame, and each page contained an illustration. As I stood there, a reproduction of two Egyptian statues appeared; they were, I think, Mycerinus and his queen. Something about their mathe-matical perfection excited me, and I stood staring. The page turned again; this time it was a photograph of a black basalt statue of a seated man; its form was so abstract that it was almost cubical in shape; the knees and the pedestal were covered with hieroglyphics. Again, the excitement made me tremble; I stared at it as if I could eat it; then the page turned again.

I walked away, possessed by a vision of mathematical per-
fection that was nevertheless wrought from living material.[5]

It is such experiences, as well as his desire for a certain
degree of material comfort and security, that leads Harry, with
Doreen, to the house of Ricky Prelati and out of James's 'league
for mutual support'. Part One of the novel ends with Harry in
Prelati's house, smoking marijuana for the first time; his initial
euphoria gives way to something else, after he has taken
sodium bicarbonate to calm an upset stomach:

> I opened the window wide, and leaned out into the night.
> The wind was cold. From somewhere nearby I could hear
> music—someone was playing the prelude to *Rheingold* with the
> window wide open. From where I was leaning, I could see the
> lighted window of the room next door, and the jiving figures;
> but the jazz was hardly audible. I realized what Oswald
> Blichstein meant when he said life was absurd. These figures
> were human beings enjoying themselves and forgetting the
> strange and paradoxical destiny of man. Yet through the glass,
> they were parodies of people, like the distorted sketches of
> Toulouse-Lautrec . . . All motion was absurd—except perhaps
> the motion of a pen across a sheet of paper, the silent motion of
> a Balzac concentrated on a great design. . . .
> The marihuana intoxication had subsided, leaving only a
> slight disgust. The kind of muzzy happiness it created was the
> enemy of incisive thought and feeling.[6]

This is the culmination of Harry's rejection of a mode of
freedom which, although attractive in some ways, depends on
indiscipline, simple hedonism and irresponsibility. Although
Wilson has said that *Adrift in Soho* was 'intended to be an
English "beat" novel', the attitude to the 'beat' way of life it
expresses is far more detached and critical than that of, say,
Jack Kerouac. *Adrift* is a novel that could have been studied
with profit by those who were drawn to the hippie movement
in the later '60s.

In the much shorter second part of the novel, the narrative
pace slows down slightly, as Harry separates himself from
James and finds another tutor: Ricky Prelati. Prelati is a
larger-than-life figure, the model of the dedicated artist, an
example who appeals to Harry's deepest impulses. James
seeks freedom by giving himself wholly to the moment; Prelati

by trying to rise above the moment. He seeks vertical freedom.
Harry realizes that he does not yet have Prelati's sense of
purpose and artistic confidence; but Prelati is an image of
what he wants to become. Even Prelati finds, however, that
the moment is not so easy to escape; Wilson gives us a comic
picture of the dedicated artist in the modern world, harassed
by admirers, bums, eager virgins, possessive older women and,
finally, the hideous roar of press and T.V.

Adrift in Soho, for all its lightness, manages to be many
things. A *Bildungsroman*; a picaresque tale; a documentary; a
period piece; a fairy story; an investigation of freedom. After
Ritual in the Dark, worked over many times, brooded on
obsessively by Wilson, it is a kind of release, a burst of lightheartedness. It also teaches a lesson relevant to Wilson's
future development as a novelist: that an apparently light-
weight form could deal with serious themes.

Adrift was followed by *The World of Violence* (1963). This is
also a first-person narrative, but the narrator is far more
detached. Like *Ritual*, *The World of Violence* is a *Bildungsroman*
with a thriller element, but it covers a much longer time-span.
Hugh Greene, a mathematician and philosopher, now aged
32, looks back on his life from the age of two to the age of 17.
The narrator's stance has a certain formality, but is essentially
leisurely and relaxed; Hugh is concerned, not only to describe,
but also to explain the events of his past and the general ideas
which they imply. With such a narrator, the expository,
didactic and moralistic tendencies evident in Harry Preston
have far wider scope. Much of *The World of Violence* consists of
summary and exposition rather than evocations of specific
scenes, and the scenes that do occur lack the careful naturalistic
detail of the previous two novels. There is little immediacy and
vivacity of presentation in the novel. It has a diagrammatic
quality, as befits the mathematician who is its ostensible
narrator. It recalls those formal intellectual autobiographies of
the nineteenth century by such men as Mill, Newman and
Ruskin; since, however, it also deals, among other things, with
violence and sex—the subjects of the sensation novels Wilson
used to read as a child—illuminating (and amusing) incon-
gruities, as well as symbolic analogies, are set up.

The first two chapters give a very entertaining account of the childhood of an exceptionally intelligent boy with less intelligent parents. It is the most intense part of the novel, but it also has some of the best comedy. In his account of the exceptional boy, Wilson no doubt intends a self-portrait to some extent, but there are important differences between character and creator. Hugh lives in a provincial town, but comes from a middle-class, not a working-class background and, whereas Wilson could find no adults to share his childhood insights and experiences, Hugh finds two kindred spirits: his Uncle Nick and his Uncle Sam. These are his unofficial, larger-than-life teachers: in inventing them, Wilson has created two excellent 'objective correlatives' for the special position of the exceptional child.

Uncle Nick discovers that the four-and-a-half-year-old Hugh is a mathematical prodigy, and becomes his private maths tutor. Soon Hugh is far closer to Nick than to his parents. As well as teaching him maths, however, Nick involves him in strange fantasies, drawn from esoteric or crank books—for example, he tells him that the earth is not one globe, but a whole series of globes, one inside the other, and that there are immense holes at the North and South Poles which run right through the centre of the earth.[7] Nick convinces Hugh that these fantasies are true, but that he must tell no-one else about them, or Nick might be murdered by mysterious 'enemies'. One day, however, Nick will be strong enough to challenge these 'enemies' openly.

All this has the effect of giving Hugh a special sense of destiny:

> here was I, at the age of seven, feeling that it would be my task, one day, to change the whole outlook of the human race. This was an awful secret to carry around. . . . I already felt responsible to the future; I was like a prince who is schooled from the age of five to the idea of becoming king. Only my task was more difficult because I had none of the prince's privileges.[8]

Suddenly, however, Nick's mind gives way completely and he spends the rest of his life in a mental home. Hugh confides in his geography teacher about Nick's fantasies; she tells the headmistress, who tells his parents. They all assure him, horrified, that all Nick's teachings were lies; but Hugh discovers that Nick's advanced mathematical tuition was sound enough.

Hugh's next teacher is his Uncle Sam, whom he meets when he is nine. Sam, when a wealthy businessman, had been overwhelmed by a sudden vision of the futility of human existence; his account of this, in the form of a 'Letter to my Nephew Hugh', is inserted into the text when Hugh begins his description of Sam, and it constitutes one of those fascinating frame tales that we will often find in Wilson's novels from now on. After his vision, Sam became a twentieth-century anchorite; he stayed permanently in a dark attic room with a bricked-up window. This is where the young Hugh meets him. Sam is, in fact, confronting the 'black room' problem: the problem of maintaining a sense of purpose and meaning in the absence of external stimuli; of gaining real, vertical freedom.

Sam recognizes Hugh as a kindred spirit and becomes, in effect, his fairy godfather; he talks to Hugh at a number of key points in the novel, gives him the money to go to London when he needs it, and eventually leaves him £20,000.

Hugh sums up the importance of Nick and Sam in this way:

> at an early age I came into contact with two men who were absolutely certain they were right and the rest of the world wrong. I had no way of judging their sanity; but from then on, I could never believe that an idea is right just because everyone accepts it.[9]

Other aspects of Hugh's intellectual development as a child are analysed—his sudden awareness of the underlying insecurity of the universe (the vastation), his sense of the stupidity of most adults—and these feed into a fascinating portrait. The emotional and instinctive world of the child has been much explored in literature, especially in the nineteenth and twentieth centuries. The intellectual world of the child has received less attention. Wilson's account of Hugh Greene's early years is an intriguing exploration of this world; an important contribution to the literature of childhood.

In *The World of Violence*, as in *Ritual in the Dark*, physical violence serves as the 'objective correlative', the physical embodiment, of the metaphysical abyss. Hugh learns of violence at an early age:

> I remember clearly a newspaper article that I read when I was very young. The journalist had been walking along a Glasgow

street when he saw a gang of men beating up a youth. He tried to interfere, and was knocked unconscious. When he opened his eyes, he found a kindly looking man bending over him, saying: 'Are you all right, son?' He said yes. The man said: 'Well next time, don't interfere in things that don't concern you', and slashed both his cheeks with a razor.[10]

Hugh is afraid of rough boys, but one day, he takes the opportunity to conquer this fear. He leads one gang of boys in an attack upon another, using his brains rather than his strength to gain victory. This frees him, temporarily, from the role of ineffectual thinker; it brings him into the 'normal' world of boyhood, without forcing him to sacrifice his intellectual superiority.

Moving on from his childhood to his teenage years, Hugh tells us that his friendship with Jeremy Wolfe, a puritanical recluse in his twenties, was the most important event of his early teens. Wolfe is, in effect, Hugh's third teacher, but he is on a smaller scale than Nick and Sam; he lacks their larger-than-life quality. But he introduces Hugh to an alternative world to that of mathematics: the world of music, philosophy, theology, the novel. This is his central significance.

While at Jeremy's cottage, Hugh senses on two occasions an occult presence—a ghost. These experiences have no follow-up in the novel; Hugh sees them as 'only a symbol of Jeremy's alien world'[11]; but it is the first definite insertion into Wilson's fictional universe of the occult—of an order of reality beneath the contingent, quotidian surface of everyday life. This idea of an underlying reality will figure centrally in the next novel we shall consider, *Man Without A Shadow*.

Hugh's discovery, through Jeremy, of an alternative world to mathematics, makes him decide against trying for a Cambridge scholarship. He leaves school at 16 and becomes a clerk with the local electricity board. He soon finds this a bore and thinks again about Cambridge; then fresh events claim his attention.

He meets Jeremy's cousin, Monty, and Monty's girlfriend, Patricia. Monty is an ex-army officer, strong and energetic, with a love of physical life; he is a passionate Don Juan. Altogether he forms a complete, almost textbook contrast to Jeremy. But despite his attractions, Patricia soon falls for

Hugh and quickly accomplishes his sexual initiation. Both Monty and Patricia are Hugh's teachers, though to a lesser extent than Jeremy; rather, they confirm Hugh's growing detachment from Jeremy. He feels that they, especially Patricia, have taught him the value of the physical life which Jeremy rejects with such fastidious disgust.

Hugh's account of his relationship with all three figures is programmatic; they are like factors in a calculation, or characters in a moral tract. The effect is like that in a Herman Hesse novel such as *Demian*—Wilson, we may note, has a great though qualified admiration for Hesse.[12] Hugh spells out the meaning of these characters. For example:

> Jeremy stood for absolute pacifism and intellectualism; Monty for a glorification of war and physical expression.[13]

The violent aspect of Monty's cult of the physical, however, leads Hugh back into 'the world of violence'. That world is epitomized for him by the leather-jacketed youths who hang around outside the local Palais de Danse, harassing and sometimes assaulting passers-by and dance-hall clients. Monty runs into a couple of them in a local pub, takes them on, and beats them; Hugh decides to follow his example, but in a more violent way. He joins the town shooting-club, buys a gun, and tries to provoke the youths to attack him; when they do, he tells himself, he will open fire. As in his childhood, with the rough boys, he wants to show that he can confront and conquer the world of violence, instead of evading it, like Jeremy. Eventually, the youths do set on him; he shoots one of them, though aiming low. At first, he fears he has killed the youth, and even when he learns he is all right, he still thinks he may be arrested. Meanwhile, Hugh has been drawn deeper into the world of crime, getting to know Kaspar, an ex-stage hypnotist who is now a crook, Jed, a simple-minded sex offender and burglar, and Dime, a pimp. In the end, Dime murders Jed, who has himself strangled a typist. In the meantime Hugh has left for London.

In *The World of Violence*, as in *Ritual in the Dark*, the *Bildungsroman* takes on some of the features of a thriller. The thriller plot that Wilson devises is ingenious, involving not only teenage violence, but also burglary, hypnosis used for criminal ends, sexual perversion and murder. Graham Greene might have made a compelling thriller out of it. With Wilson, however, its thriller potential is not fully realized. This is partly due to the lack of immediacy in the narrative; an effective thriller needs sharpness of presentation. A further reason is the detachment of the hero. Hugh is irritated by what he thinks of as the irrelevant complications of his involvement with crime. When he learns that Jed is a sex-killer, the knowledge leaves him untouched. Instead of creating suspense from the possibility that Hugh may be arrested for shooting the youth, Wilson has Hugh tell us, for instance: 'Deep inside me, I did not expect to find detectives waiting at home for me, and I was right.'[14]

We noted Sorme's detachment in *Ritual in the Dark*; in *The World of Violence*, our sense of Hugh's detachment is greater because of the more formal style and the putative distance in time of the narrator from the action.

In fact, *The World of Violence* is an anti-thriller. We are constantly directed away from the exciting possibilities of the plot towards Hugh's states of mind; his internal development and his ideas.

This has important implications for Wilson's future novels. In *Ritual in the Dark* and *The World of Violence*, the thriller element has both a structural and symbolic function: it helps to give shape to the novel and symbolizes the metaphysical abyss, the negation of values and meaning. In the earlier novel, the positive direction of the hero and the negative direction of the thriller plot were held together by the immediacy of presentation and the naturalistic detail. In *The World of Violence*, the distanced narration, the naturalistic thinness, and the subsidiary role of the thriller plot in comparison to *Ritual*, causes that plot and the story of the hero's internal development to spring apart. There are two ways of dealing with such a disjunction: to try and integrate hero and plot into a realistic whole, or to let the disjunction stand, in fact to emphasize it, while nonetheless making the novel more effective on the plot level. From *Necessary Doubt* onwards, Wilson will take the latter course.

Wilson's fourth novel, issued in the same year as *The World of Violence* (1963), was originally called *Man Without A Shadow*, but is now generally issued under a more vivid title: *The Sex Diary of Gerard Sorme*. It is, once more, primarily a *Bildungsroman*, but this time it uses the modes of an intimate 'sex diary' and an occult thriller. By adopting the diary form and the Sorme *persona*, Wilson permits himself far greater freedom than in his three previous novels. In contrast to *The World of Violence*, the narrator is not distanced in time from the events he describes, but immediately and vigorously involved in them, and he records those events, and his ideas, not in a detached, formal style, but in an aggressive, direct and uninhibited way. His ideas, unlike those in *The World of Violence*, do not seem like formal expositions, but are themselves lived experiences, existential moments that feed into the other experiences described.

At the end of the novel, Sorme notes: 'I am told that some of the aims and motives revealed in [these diaries] are hardly creditable, and that some passages are extremely damaging.'[15] Certainly this Sorme does not seem wholly agreeable, much less so than the Sorme of *Ritual* (their continuity is problematic), though Wilson does not appear to find much wrong with the Mark II version. To the reader, however, this Sorme emerges as arrogant, self-willed, self-regarding, insensitive, impatient, intolerant; in some ways he resembles 'Huggett' in Angus Wilson's short story 'A Bit Off The Map'—a satirical portrait of Colin Wilson.[16] Nonetheless, his raw energy, his will-to-power, his honesty compel our interest and sometimes our admiration. He bears some likeness, especially in his sexual concerns, to the 'I' of Henry Miller's novels; but there are important differences.

Sorme's main quest is, of course, Wilson's: how to achieve a sustained intensity of consciousness. This time, Sorme's researches take him into two main fields: sexuality and the occult. The two meet in the person of Caradoc Cunningham, with his practice of 'sexual magic'. Cunningham is another of Wilson's larger-than-life 'teachers'. In Cunningham's character, as in Austin Nunne's, there are suggestions of cruelty; but in contrast to Nunne, he is essentially comic. As in *Ritual*, however, Sorme learns from his teacher but eventually rejects him.

The first hundred pages of the novel, up to Sorme's meeting with Cunningham, focus on sexuality, combining Sorme's sexual theories with a montage of vivid anecdotes about his past and present sexual experiences. Sorme's central claim is that sex is a means of achieving the experience of power, meaning and purpose; well before he meets Cunningham, he himself draws the analogy between sex and magic:

> Of one thing I am certain. The sexual force is the nearest thing to magic—to the supernatural—that human beings ever experience. It deserves perpetual and close study. No study is so profitable to the philosopher. In the sex force, he can watch the purpose of the universe in action.[17]

But this exalted view does not make Sorme an idealizing sexual mystic. He is well aware of other aspects of sexuality. The sordid, for instance:

> I think of a red-haired boy called Barrett who talked of nothing but sex. One day, I heard two of his friends laughing about him. They had been to the theatre the night before, and in the 'gods' had picked up three little girls. Barrett had disappeared into a back street with his girl; when his friends went to look for him, he was having sex against a dustbin. They called to him, but he was apparently unable to stop. The boys imitated his motion obscenely, jerking the hips back and forward like a dog with a mechanical motion. This stuck in my mind for a long time—sex as the force that turned men into dogs. The worst of it was that, even so, I envied Barrett.[18]

Sorme is strongly conscious as well of a link between sex and violence—a link that Hugh Greene had also come to recognize early.[19] He recalls a number of incidents where he has been very excited by a woman precisely because it was difficult to possess her; conversely, a freely available woman has sometimes left him cold. These are examples of Wilson's 'theory of symbolic response', which we looked at in Chapter Two. Sexual response is directed by the imagination, and the imagination is aroused by symbols of the forbidden, the unattainable; the sexual impulse becomes a desire to break taboos, to overpower; it fuses with aggression. Sorme recalls accidentally catching sight of a woman in her underwear in the changing-room of a clothes shop.

> If I had found the woman in my bed, I doubt whether I'd have been able to summon the appetite to take her. And yet I recognized that the intensity of desire I felt could easily drive a man to murder and rape. I am, I hope, incapable of either, and yet I

was trembling with excitement—an unhealthy, burning excitement that does no good. As I passed other girls in the street, women returning from offices, I felt: all these women have this same capacity to arouse this feeling hidden below this opaque outer layer of clothing. Our society is sitting on a sexual powder-barrel.[20]

Sorme stresses that he does not think his sexual response exceptional:

I believe that, far from being 'abnormal', the intensity of my sexual impulse is a part of the total intensity that makes me what I am—an intelligent being, responding with unusual directness to the problems of modern civilization.[21]

But despite Sorme's concern with sex, he rejects it as an ultimate end. He comments on a friend's love of seduction:

I honestly believe he could devote his life to the pursuit of women, like Casanova, finding in each one a new universe. He's an example of the sexual illusion at its most intense—and in many ways, at its best.[22]

Monty in *The World of Violence* is similarly enthralled by this 'illusion'. For Sorme, however, sex is only one means to the experience of power, meaning, and purpose.

Man Without A Shadow, by dramatizing Wilson's view of sexuality with particular vivacity, invites us to question it more strongly than any of his other novels (except perhaps *The God of the Labyrinth*). We noted in Chapter Three that Wilson showed little interest in personal relationships in his novels; this is especially clear when he writes about sex. Women are not people, but means to the end of orgasm; Wilson has himself commented that his women characters are all 'amateur prostitutes' and it has been suggested that all the sexual encounters in his novels could be summed up in the phrase: 'Then I took off her pants.'[33] The idea that sexual response may be linked to the quality of a relationship and that the relationship may provide symbols which complexify and subtilize that response is largely absent.

To some extent, this could be put down to Wilson's belief in the impersonality of sex; the belief expressed by Don Juan in Shaw's *Man and Superman*:

73

> *Don Juan:* Do my sex the justice to admit, Senora, that we
> have always recognized that the sex relation is not a personal or
> friendly relation at all.
> *Ana:* Not a personal or friendly relation! What relation is
> more personal? more sacred? more holy?
> *Don Juan:* Sacred and holy, if you like, Ana, but not personally
> friendly. Your relation to God is sacred and holy: dare you call it
> personally friendly? In the sex relation the universal creative
> energy, of which the parties are both the helpless agents, over-
> rides and sweeps away all personal considerations and dispenses
> with all personal relations.[24]

Ana comments: 'we know the libertine's philosophy' and it
could be argued that Sorme's view of sex is highly personal
insofar as orgasm seems to be a means to enhance his sense of
personal power and control. The self, the will, is not left
behind at the bedroom door, but exalted. This emphasis on
aggression and the will-to-power conveys a certain truth about
sex, one which has perhaps been neglected in those theories,
widespread today, which view sex as harmless pleasure, or
integrally bound up with love and loss of self. But it is a partial
truth.

The occult is Sorme's other main field of interest in *Man
Without A Shadow*. In the first part of the novel, it is mentioned
indirectly. Sorme more than once draws the kind of analogy
between sex and magic we have noted. Furthermore, there are
hints of a hidden order of reality between apparently random
everyday events. Early in the novel, for instance, Sorme buys
Gorky's memoir of Tolstoy:

> I find on the title page of the Gorky this comment by Tolstoy:
> 'The flesh rages and riots, and the spirit follows it, helpless and
> miserable.' This was the first thing I saw when I opened the
> book, the subject that had been foremost in my mind for days.
> Are these things chance? They incline me to believe that the
> world has its own secret motives and intentions.[25]

The themes both of magic, and of the non-contingent reality
that magic symbolizes, are developed as the novel progresses.
Their fusion with the theme of sexuality is embodied in
Caradoc Cunningham. Appropriately, Sorme first sees Cunningham 'by chance'. He is reading in a public library when
he sees a big, bald man approach a library assistant, disappear

with her to the basement and return ten minutes later. Although Sorme finds it difficult to believe, he feels that the man, in that short time, has seduced the girl, though they seemed to be total strangers. Later, quite unexpectedly, Sorme is introduced to Cunningham when he looks up Oliver Glasp again; Glasp had got to know Cunningham quite independently. These 'chance' encounters are, in one respect, flagrant coincidences, breaches of the realistic convention; but they serve to reinforce the idea that 'the world has its own secret motives and intentions'.

Wilson's portrait of Cunningham is based largely on the real-life magician, Aleister Crowley (1875–1947).[26] Cunningham is big, bald, has bulging eyes; he gives an impression of power and weakness, of being both a charlatan and a man of sincere vision. He is a magician, an adventurer, a sexually versatile seducer, a con-man, a bad poet, a mountaineer. In Sorme's words, he has 'the vitality of ten men and the audacity of fifty' and 'more than a touch of greatness'.[27]

The second part of the novel focuses on Sorme's friendship with Cunningham. Along the way, Sorme also succeeds in wooing and winning Diana, the wife of an eccentric composer who lives in the room below him. But this is a subsidiary matter; as always in Wilson's novels, the central relationships, those on which the novelist concentrates, are between men; though the hero may affirm the importance of the woman in his life, the second sex takes second place.

As with Nunne in *Ritual in the Dark*, Sorme gradually builds up a picture of Cunningham, from talking with him, from hearing others talk of him, from thinking about him. Cunningham's affirmations of optimism, of an immense faith in life, arouse a strong positive response; but from others, he hears tales of Cunningham's callousness and cruelty. While not wholly convinced by these, he realizes that they have affected his image of Cunningham, 'made me see him in a different way, as a weakling'.[28]

Cunningham's main interest is magic, and he tries to convince Sorme of its value—especially of the value of 'sexual magic' as a means of prolonging the orgasm and the insights it brings. Sorme is highly sceptical. Cunningham tries to demonstrate various paranormal powers that he claims to possess;

Sorme remains unconvinced, but nonetheless acknowledges that he finds the 'possibility of developing new powers immensely exciting'.[29]

Sorme attends and assists at two of Cunningham's magical ceremonies. In his account of these, he is interested but detached and sceptical. Thus a comic effect is produced, a spoof of Dennis Wheatley. In the first ceremony, Cunningham purports to battle with enemies who are threatening him with occult forces; in the second, he attempts to demonstrate his 'sexual magic'. During this demonstration, Sorme falls asleep and wakes up the next morning to find that Carlotta, one of the girls taking part, has been taken to hospital after drinking too much of a supposed aphrodisiac. A newspaper scandal follows, and extracts from Sorme's 'sex diary', which the Press have got hold of, are published. To escape publicity, Cunningham disappears to America, and Sorme, with Diana, to Ireland.

Despite the farce of the ending and the comic aspect of Cunningham, Sorme's development in *Man Without A Shadow* has been a serious one, towards an increasingly strong definition of a purpose that is not merely personal, but evolutionary. As he says himself: 'I am evolution made conscious.'[30] Growing with this evolutionary consciousness is his awareness of an order beneath the apparently random surface of the day-to-day world. One feature of this awareness is a belief in the possibility of occult powers. Sorme continues to want his ' "richness" to be natural, not supernatural', but comes to feel that the occult may offer some insights into intensifying consciousness and into the hidden web of relationships in the universe.[31]

In this chapter, we have looked at three novels which are very different from each other in some ways, but also have much in common. There is the detachment of the hero from the action in *Adrift in Soho* and *The World of Violence*, and, despite the greater immediacy of the diary form, in *Man Without A Shadow* to some extent, for example in Sorme's account of the magical ceremonies. There is a growing belief in a non-contingent reality underlying the everyday world, which is conveyed both by direct statement and by a free-and-easy use of coincidence, especially in *Man Without A Shadow*. Linked with that belief is a qualified but definite interest in the occult—playing a minor role in *The World of Violence*, but much more prominent in *Man Without A*

Shadow. There is a frank use of popular elements, without the concern for credibility we found in *Ritual in the Dark*: the thriller plot in *The World of Violence*, the black magic aspect of *Man Without A Shadow*. There is a growing clarification of Wilson's ideas, an increasing readiness to present them by direct exposition and, in *Man Without A Shadow*, an emphasis on their evolutionary implications. All these features crystallize in Wilson's later novels.

As we move on to those novels, we should also remember this. In the fiction we have looked at so far, Wilson has drawn heavily upon his personal experience as well as on his reading and imagination. *Ritual in the Dark* and *Adrift in Soho* owe a good deal to Wilson's days in 1950s London. *The World of Violence* draws, though often indirectly, on his childhood and adolescence in Leicester. *Man Without A Shadow* uses autobiographical material, including, at the end, Wilson's own experience of a 'sex diary' scandal.[32] But, as we saw in Chapter One, Wilson's life, after his retreat from London in 1957, took on an even, quiet tenor. His later novels reflect this in that they rely less on personal experience than on reading and imagination.

Wilson would argue that this does not represent an evasion of life but a drive towards a deeper life, beneath the empirical, everyday world. It might seem to pose problems for him as a novelist, however, since the novel has been identified closely, though by no means exclusively, with the empirical, everyday world. In recent years, however, we have become much more conscious that the novel, like all literary forms, is a matter of conventions; realism, the focus on the empirical and everyday, is only one of its conventions, though an especially prominent one. But there is no reason why a novel should not use other conventions; in fact, there is a large group of novels that are not primarily realistic: popular novels. We have seen how Wilson's early reading taught him that popular fiction could act as an imaginative stimulus and symbolize serious concerns; we have explored the popular elements in his first four novels. Now we will see how his later novels primarily employ, not the conventions of realism (*The Killer* is a special case), but those of popular fiction.

NOTES

1. 'Note', *God of the Labyrinth*, p. 283.
2. *Adrift in Soho* (Gollancz, 1961; my refs. to Boston, Houghton Mifflin ed., 1961), p. 14.
3. *Adrift*, p. 142.
4. *Adrift*, p. 89.
5. *Adrift*, pp. 73–4.
6. *Adrift*, pp. 164–65.
7. As Hugh later discovers (*The World of Violence*, Gollancz, 1963, pp. 29–30), Uncle Nick's ideas owe something to Paul Jackson Caine's *The Hollow Earth*.
8. *Violence*, p. 19.
9. *Violence*, p. 43.
10. *Violence*, p. 47.
11. *Violence*, p. 90.
12. *Outsider*, pp. 61–78. *Hesse, Reich, Borges*.
13. *Violence*, p. 113.
14. *Violence*, p. 214.
15. *Man Without A Shadow*, p. 251.
16. Cf. 'Huggett says that it's more the Will. We've got to breed a new race with real Will Power. It's Will Power that'll get you to the top.' Angus Wilson, 'A Bit Off The Map' in *A Bit Off The Map* (Secker & Warburg, 1957; my ref. to Granada, 1982 ed.), pp. 13–14.
17. *Shadow*, p. 25.
18. *Shadow*, p. 25.
19. See *Violence*, pp. 158–59.
20. *Shadow*, p. 28.
21. *Shadow*, p. 28.
22. *Shadow*, pp. 25–6.
23. Wilson made the 'amateur prostitutes' comment in an interview with Timothy Wilson, *Guardian* (24 May 1971). I am indebted to Mr. Philip Burrows for the 'Then I took off her pants' observation.
24. *Man and Superman*, p. 125.
25. *Shadow*, p. 48.
26. Chapter 7 of *Occult*, 'The Beast Himself', deals with Aleister Crowley.
27. *Shadow*, pp. 129, 153.
28. *Shadow*, p. 177.
29. *Shadow*, p. 137.
30. *Shadow*, p. 86. Italics in original.
31. *Shadow*, p. 166.
32. See *Voyage*, pp. 134–36. *World of Colin Wilson*, pp. 129–31.

6

Unofficial Detectives: *Necessary Doubt* and *The Glass Cage*

Necessary Doubt (1964) is the first of Wilson's out-and-out popular form novels. It is a detective thriller, with a science-fiction twist at the end. In contrast to *Ritual in the Dark* and *The World of Violence*, the thriller plot is not assimilated to a larger whole, but provides the overall structure of the novel.

Karl Zweig is a 65-year-old 'existential theologian'. Austrian by birth, he now lives in London. One day, from a taxi, he catches a glimpse of a man he has not seen for many years: Gustav Neumann. Neumann's father was a close friend of Zweig's; Zweig watched Neumann grow up, and Neumann became his student in philosophy. Like Wittgenstein, Neumann was brilliant, but unstable; after a series of escapades, he told Zweig that he intended to become a 'great criminal'. Soon afterwards, to escape the Nazis, Neumann and his father left Germany for Switzerland, while Zweig, then teaching in Germany, left for America. Zweig has lost touch with Neumann since then; but he has sometimes heard curious reports of him acting as secretary or nurse to rich, elderly men who have died in mysterious circumstances. Now, Zweig learns, he is the companion of Sir Timothy Ferguson—another rich, elderly man. With his friend Sir Charles Grey, an ex-head of the C.I.D., Zweig sets out to investigate. They are joined by Joseph Atholl Gardner, a writer of highly speculative ('crank') books

79

on such topics as Atlantis and the ten lost tribes of Israel, and by Natasha, Gardner's younger, attractive wife. As this unlikely crew proceed with their investigation of what Grey calls 'the craziest murder case I've ever been on', it seems more and more likely that Neumann is a multiple murderer.[1] Zweig, however, feels a growing reluctance to have Neumann caught. Like Sorme with Nunne in *Ritual in the Dark*, Zweig determines to talk to Neumann before the police, who are steadily closing the net, reach him. But it is Neumann who comes to Zweig. He gives him a drug which produces a greatly enhanced state of consciousness. Although uncertain that Neumann is completely innocent, Zweig, as Sherlock Holmes sometimes did, waives legal process in favour of a more personal conception of justice. With Gardner's assistance, he agrees to help Neumann escape to France, and to join him in his researches into intensifying consciousness.

Necessary Doubt is much more exciting as a thriller than *Ritual in the Dark* or *The World of Violence*. This is because the metaphysical and the thriller elements are co-extensive; they work alongside and feed into each other. The mystery about Neumann is sustained to the end and, in one sense, it is the same on both the thriller and metaphysical levels—is Neumann a multiple murderer?—although the implications on each level are, of course, different. Zweig's curiosity and sense of urgency match the detective urgency in their pace and focus, although they also diverge from the detective quest in their underlying concerns. In this use of a detective thriller to symbolize and explore metaphysical issues, Wilson has acknowledged a debt to the Swiss writer, Friedrich Dürrenmatt.[2]

Zweig is not the essentially optimistic, self-confident hero of Wilson's earlier novels. He is uncertain and self-questioning: a practitioner of necessary doubt. In contrast to, for instance, Hugh in *The World of Violence*, he lacks a basic certainty that he will come through successfully in the end. He is, in his way, at risk—metaphysical risk—while the mystery of Neumann persists, and it persists, though with modifications, even at the end of the novel.

The creation of character is not the main object of *Necessary Doubt*; the conventions of the thriller militate against the production of 'rounded' characters. Sir Charles Grey is a stock figure; Joseph Gardner has comic possibilities, but is sketchily drawn. The characterization of Zweig, however, though not fully developed, is successful. Wilson does especially well in conveying Zweig's sense of himself as ageing, growing tired:

> It was his usual practice to read for a few minutes before turning off the light; this evening, he opened the photograph album again and turned over the pages. Looking at a picture of himself in battledress, it suddenly seemed incredible that he was now an old man, with perhaps only another ten years to live. Forty years had passed like a dream, leaving as little behind; a few memories, a little achievement—and the wall of mist ahead, as inscrutable as his beginnings. He thought: Strange how my sense of reality changes. In youth, everything is too real; towards the end, nothing is real.[3]

Zweig also has a representative quality. His biography encapsulates an important strand of twentieth-century Western culture. He comes from that central European matrix which has produced so much of cultural value, but which has also become associated, in our time, with the darkest examples of man's inhumanity to man. Before the war, Zweig taught at Heidelberg University and knew the philosophers Jaspers, Heidegger and Cassirer. He tells Natasha:

> [In] Germany after the first war [it] seemed to many of us that the world had entered a new era. We were all pacifists. We saw the wreckage of Europe around us, but this seemed a guarantee that no one would ever dare to start another war. We all believed that Geneva would be the symbol of a new world of reason and co-operation. . . .
> [Cassirer and I] saw a Europe like ancient Athens, but without the cowards and the assassins, without the corruption and petty nationalism . . . And then came Hitler. It was sudden and unbelievable, like the Vandals on Rome. And there was Spengler, with his message that the West is dying because civilization is like any flower that has to die. We could hardly believe it. The night was back again.[4]

This disillusionment turned Zweig into a Christian. He exemplifies a widespread twentieth-century pattern: optimism for the human future based, at least partly, on political grounds, followed by disillusionment and the recourse to a traditional world-view. A similar pattern is evident in the lives of those who fought what they believed to be 'the war to end war', and those who saw hope, during the 1930s, in Communism.

Now Zweig lives comfortably. He has settled in England; his books sell well; he is academically respectable; he has a small popular reputation, occasionally appearing on a T.V. programme called 'Ask the Experts'. He is, in Wilson's terms, very much an 'Insider'—and a victim of the 'age of defeat'.

Necessary Doubt is primarily the story of Zweig's regeneration, in which the possibility of a more general regeneration of Western culture is implied. It is no mere detective hunt that Zweig is engaged on, but a quest for spiritual revival; his hunt for Neumann is a hunt for the 'New Man'. The action of the novel takes place over a cold, snowy Christmas; the wintry weather, of which we are frequently made aware, complements our sense of a certain sterility in Zweig which Wilson's evocation of his age and essential solitude has aroused. Christmas, for both pagan and Christian, is a symbol of spiritual rebirth in the heart of winter. For Wilson, it is also one of those moments when consciousness expands, and the world seems richer, stranger, more meaningful. *Necessary Doubt* could be called Wilson's *Christmas Carol*. It is the story of a conversion, like Dickens's tale, but in reverse; not to Christianity, but from Christianity to evolutionary existentialism.

Zweig's regeneration is due centrally to his quest for, and encounters with, Neumann. Once Neumann's teacher, he now becomes his pupil; in this respect, *Necessary Doubt*, though its central character is an old man, is, like the novels before it, a *Bildungsroman*, and Neumann is another larger-than-life teacher. Zweig's relationship to Neumann has some affinities with that of Sorme and Nunne in *Ritual in the Dark*, but, in an important respect, it has a reverse movement. Zweig, like Sorme with Nunne, is fascinated by Neumann; in Neumann, as in Nunne, though less strongly, there are suggestions of brutality and ruthlessness; Zweig, like Sorme, finds himself defending a possible multiple murderer and, in the end, helping him to escape the police. But in *Ritual*, Sorme starts out as Nunne's friend and admirer, gradually discovers that he may be a murderer, finally confirms this and, although conniving at his escape from the police, rejects him as, essentially, a self-destructive failure. In *Necessary Doubt*, by contrast, Zweig starts out as a hunter—though his motivation is, of course, never a simple 'detective' one—feels increasing sympathy and respect for Neumann and, eventually, joins forces with him. His conclusion is that Neumann, although he may not be wholly innocent, is, unlike Nunne, a man of genuine strength and vision, sincerely pursuing the evolutionary quest.

In *Necessary Doubt*, we do not at first meet Neumann directly, as we meet Nunne in *Ritual*. In fact, it is not until over a third of the way through the book that we encounter him face-to-face. Nonetheless, he is the absent focus of our attention. We see him in brief, tantalizing glimpses, and through what Zweig says about him—especially in the account that Zweig gives to Sir Charles Grey and his wife. This account constitutes the first part of a major frame tale within the novel: a compressed *Bildungsroman* dealing with the early life and development of Gustav Neumann. It is a fascinating story.

Neumann was a highly intelligent but withdrawn boy, closely attached to his mother. She died when he was 10, and he was deeply affected. His father took him travelling abroad, and when Gustav came back, 'something had hardened inside him.'[5] Gustav was Jewish, and argued that the Jews were too passive and should defend themselves against anti-Semitism, which was growing in Germany at that time, by violence if necessary. When Gustav was 13, Ernst Junger, the leader of an anti-Semitic gang at the private school Gustav attended, was scalded in a school shower. Neumann indicated to Zweig that he fixed the shower to make this happen. When Zweig asked what would have happened if another boy had been scalded by mistake, Neumann replied: 'It would have been a pity. I would have thought of some other method of revenge on Junger.'[6]

Neumann became Zweig's pupil when he was 18. By then, he was less withdrawn, apparently because of his close friendship with a youth called Georgi Braunschweig. Braunschweig was often ill, and after an anti-Semitic beating, in which Junger may have been involved, he died. After this, Neumann attempted suicide. Then he became sullen and withdrawn, but dedicated himself to his academic studies and became Zweig's most brilliant pupil. In 1930, a book by Zweig called *End of an Epoch* was published. Neumann read it straight through, then came at once to see Zweig. They talked from two o'clock till dawn. Recalling this, Zweig remarks on 'the extraordinary depth of [Neumann's] *feeling* about philosophy. He seemed to be tortured by the problem of why men are alive.'[7] For Wilson, this urgent existential need is the starting point of any worthwhile philosophy. Zweig's talk with Neumann made him feel that Neumann might 'well be one of the great thinkers of our age'.[8]

Neumann began to consolidate his intellectual reputation; he published a brilliant paper on phenomenology. Then he read another new book by Zweig: *Necessary Doubt*. This argued that man's capacity to doubt is his greatest dignity. The idea seemed to bring out a nihilistic streak in Neumann; he began to drink heavily and show other signs of instability; once, he stole a Rolls-Royce, and let it run over a cliff. A further publication of Zweig's provoked his greatest crisis yet, however.

This publication was an article in which Zweig argued that the philosopher should grasp truth, not by analytic thought, but in sudden moments of vision; moreover, he contended that closeness to death could bring such moments. When he had read this, Neumann came to Zweig in a highly excitable state; he told him that, at first, the article had made him decide to commit suicide. Then he had decided to go and see Heidegger in Freiburg and ask him why, given his claim that man knows reality only in the face of death, he did not kill himself at once. To prove his sincerity, he would shoot himself in front of Heidegger. There is a note of black comedy in this; in later life, Neumann will write:

> In spite of its unpleasantness, there is something humorous about suicide. As an evaluation of life, it has some of the quality of a schoolboy howler.[9]

At this stage, he is incapable of the detachment which would enable him to find anything funny in his feelings; but the humour is evident to the reader. So, however, are the possible serious consequences.

On the train to Freiburg, Neumann changed his plan once more. He had a vision of the human race as worthless insects and decided to kill himself there and then. But two fat, complacent bankers sitting opposite him aroused his anger, and he felt like killing them instead. Then his 'great idea' came to him:

> I'd found the answer—to be a criminal, a master criminal. All human beings are insects, and the gods laugh at us. There's nothing we can do to become great. . . . What *can* a man do to try to be more than an insect? What could he do so that the gods would say: 'He is different from the others?' The answer is: take the side of the gods against human beings. Try to be a real criminal, the first criminal in the history of the human race who is not just an underprivileged victim. . . .[10]

Thus Neumann seems destined for destructiveness. He could kill himself or others; go mad; adopt some extreme political creed. He exemplifies decadent late European Romanticism, especially as manifested in 'the Germany of brutality and decadence, the Germany that swayed like a snake to the music that spoke of suicide and death'.[11]

That was Zweig's final meeting with Neumann. It left him with an enigma; and it is this which draws him, in old age, back to Neumann's trail. The enigma is not primarily on the 'detective' level, however:

> If . . . Neumann proved to be a second Landru, Zweig would be disappointed and saddened. What excited him was a prospect that he was unwilling to define because it seemed too unlikely; but it was connected with his final conversation with . . . Neumann in Heidelberg.[12]

Zweig and his companions track Neumann down to a cottage near Bury St. Edmunds, where he is staying with Sir Timothy Ferguson; he is supposed to be Ferguson's secretary. Grey and Gardner keep watch on the cottage, while Zweig and Natasha go to look round the town. When they get back to their hotel, Zweig and Natasha find Neumann waiting for them. The quarry has sought out his hunters.

Their encounter is a core scene of *Necessary Doubt*. It has a density which comes from both its immediate richness and its focusing of key themes in the novel. The tension, the ambivalence, the peculiar quality of the encounter are strikingly conveyed. In confronting Neumann, Zweig is confronting his own past, his neglected possibilities, which are also the past and neglected possibilities of a culture. Neumann forces him to examine his present self in relation to these.

Neumann is no longer the unstable young man Zweig recalled, alternately wild and sullen. He is exceptionally calm and self-possessed; that makes him even more enigmatic and disturbing. He gives nothing away; he refuses to meet Zweig on equal terms; he is rude with cool, controlled effectiveness. In this scene we, like Zweig, do not know what to make of him; and this ambiguity, though with a different emphasis, remains on a re-reading, because even at the end of the novel, Neumann is still an ambivalent figure. His main function in this scene, however, is to present a direct challenge to Zweig; his rudeness, to a man accustomed, as Zweig is, to respect, is part of the challenge. Like a Zen teacher, Neumann uses shock tactics which disrupt fixed perceptions. For example, he says to Zweig:

> You urge me to be frank. Very well, and I hope you will not be offended. There were certain German philosophers and artists who were criticized for remaining in Germany and supporting the Nazis—Heidegger, for example. Others preferred to leave the country and gain a reputation as martyrs. . . . You were one of those who went to America and became a symbol of humanitarianism. So not many people were surprised when you declared yourself a Christian. But I could remember your telling my father that only a fool, a knave or a weakling could be a Christian in our century. . . . I agreed with what you said at the time, and I still agree with it. There is only one thing I would like to know. Which of the three do you think you have become?[13]

Zweig's discomfiture at Neumann's challenges is not merely that of a polite man confronted by rudeness. Its deeper cause is that Neumann's words strike home; they are contributing, painfully, to his old teacher's regeneration.

Zweig does not meet Neumann face-to-face again until the end of the book; but Neumann, absent, remains a potent presence, ambivalent, challenging, compelling. Zweig's obsession with Neumann is both cause and effect of a change in himself.

Zweig's relationship with Gardner's wife, Natasha, also contributes to this change, though less fundamentally. Wilson has been accused of spicing his books with sex to increase his sales—*Man Without A Shadow*, especially with its newer title, is obviously an important exhibit in this case—but, as one of his defenders has pointed out, several of his novels have little or no sex, and the text of *Necessary Doubt* is exceptionally chaste.[14] Though Zweig's relationship with Natasha has undoubted sexual undertones, it involves hardly any physical contact. Wilson's account of the relationship is delicate, economical, sometimes very amusing, and, in the end, curiously moving. Its contribution to Zweig's regeneration is emphasized when, near the end of the novel, with the police closing in on Neumann, Zweig tells Natasha that he owes both her and Neumann the same thing: 'a feeling of being alive again'.[15] Finally, however, Natasha feels, and Zweig inwardly agrees, that she has 'lost' him to Neumann. The most important relationship in a Wilson novel once again turns out to be that of men linked by a common quest.

Zweig's final encounter with Neumann completes his regeneration. As with the scene at the hotel, it is the hunted who seeks out the hunter. Neumann takes Zweig to a cottage in Egham owned by Sir Timothy Ferguson. We may recall in *Ritual*, the final confrontation between Nunne and Sorme in an isolated cottage. Then, Nunne confirmed that he was a multiple murderer; now, Neumann is to assert his innocence. This is near the end of the novel, the point at which, in a traditional detective story, 'all is revealed.' Here, however, the detective revelation is less important than the metaphysical revelation. But not everything is cleared up, on either plane; uncertainties—necessary doubts—remain.

First of all, Neumann gives Zweig a drug: neuromysin. The effect is remarkable:

> His brain felt like an electric generator working a searchlight; his body and flesh seemed realler than usual, somehow controllable, his own, not a casual extension of himself.[16]

Wilson is not, however, offering a Huxleyan parable on the joys of drugtaking. He has made it clear, for example in his account of his own mescalin experience, that he believes drugs sap the will and self-discipline which are so important in his model of evolutionary man.[17] This point is driven home in the novel. When Zweig tells Neumann that he has produced a drug which could alter the course of world history, Neumann replies:

> you are mistaken. Neuromysin produces this effect on you because you have a highly disciplined mind. . . . Even so, you now show signs of strain and overexcitement. Imagine what would happen if a completely undisciplined person took the drug. His mind would be like a zoo with all the cages open— total chaos. His excitement would burn out the motor of his brain.[18]

Wilson uses the idea of neuromysin not to advocate drug-taking, but to symbolize the enlargement of consciousness that should one day be attainable by will-power. Here, the detective thriller becomes a science fiction tale as well—and, in using a science fiction device to symbolize the 'evolutionary leap', *Necessary Doubt* anticipates *The Philosopher's Stone* with its 'Neumann alloy'.

As Zweig marvels at the effect of neuromysin, Neumann talks to him at length about his life and researches, which have been conducted, as R. H. W. Dillard puts it, 'on the fringes of legality and morality'.[19] He is, in fact, continuing the *Bildungsroman* begun by Zweig's account of Neumann at the start of the novel. He is, also, assuming the role of teacher to his old professor, but not by the shock tactics he adopted on their previous encounter; now he treats Zweig with respect. Like the final meeting between Nunne and Sorme, this meeting is a kind of trial: an existential trial in which Neumann, like Nunne, conducts his own defence, a defence that Zweig has been conducting for him until now, as Sorme, in *Ritual*, conducted the defence of Nunne.

Neumann tells Zweig that he long ago abandoned the idea of becoming a 'great criminal'. He offers innocent explanations of the deaths of the elderly men for whom he worked. He explains how he worked with his father on research into drugs; he tells Zweig: 'I wanted a drug to create the superman.'[20] Eventually, his father discovered a drug called neurocaine; the drug, by destroying habit patterns, produced an initial feeling of euphoria, but mental collapse followed; this led to his father's suicide. Neumann, however, continued his researches, working completely alone; now, he asks Zweig to join him, telling him: 'I shall need your help.'[21] Zweig agrees. In his old age, he has been converted again; evolutionary quest succeeds Christian quiescence.

Zweig's course in *Necessary Doubt* has been a 'voyage to a beginning', to the point where his quest becomes a consciously evolutionary one. We had seen something of this in Gerard Sorme in *Man Without A Shadow*; but in the later novel, it is stressed by Zweig's re-conversion. More exactly than in any of Wilson's previous fiction, *Necessary Doubt* symbolizes the movement from existence to evolution. It also conveys the ambivalence of the evolutionary quest; the pursuit of the superhuman involves, if not an indiscriminate contempt for the human, certainly a severance from the ordinary world which is painful, even terrifying. As he listens to Neumann's account of his early drug experiments:

> Zweig felt obscurely revolted, not by Neumann's description of his experiment, but by something more dangerous. The life in him squirmed away from some realization, as from a cold wind.[22]

This ambivalence is focused on Neumann himself, in the suggestions of brutality and ruthlessness, of a certain inhumanity, about him. Even at the end of the novel, after Neumann has made his case for the defence to Zweig, this is not dispelled; Zweig admits to Natasha that he is not fully convinced of Neumann's innocence:

> I believe this: that Gustav has never ceased to be possessed by a vision of his own, and that he has spent his life trying to turn it into a reality. I doubt whether he set out simply to kill these men for money—he is not interested in money. I think that perhaps he hoped to help them. But I think he used them as guinea pigs. . . .[23]

Nevertheless, he gives Neumann the benefit of the doubt; it is necessary, in the interests of human evolution.

For Wilson, *Necessary Doubt* represents the discovery of a method towards which he has been working, with varying degrees of consciousness, in his previous novels. This method is the one described in Chapter Three: the use of a popular fictional form—perhaps with elements from other popular forms mixed in—to structure and symbolize an investigation of his deepest preoccupations. It will be the method he follows in subsequent novels. As well as its structural and symbolic functions, the popular form method constitutes also an attempt to bridge the gap between serious and popular fiction that Wilson dislikes.

Necessary Doubt, furthermore, encapsulates Wilson's progress from an existential to an evolutionary position. The ambivalence of the novel is fundamentally due to Zweig's uncertainty about whether to commit himself to the evolutionary quest; in the end, he decides to do so. His commitment is also Wilson's. Significantly, a science fiction device is used to symbolize Zweig's conversion to evolutionism; science fiction will become more important in Wilson's later novels. All of those novels, whether in science fiction form or not, will reflect a new certainty about the hidden order of reality, a firmer faith in man's untapped powers.

This new certainty is evident in *The Glass Cage* (1966). Like *Necessary Doubt*, this novel uses the form of the detective story as a structuring and symbolic device; the hero, like Karl Zweig, is an unlikely unofficial detective, a leading Blake scholar called Damon Reade. Zweig, however, in the course of *Necessary Doubt*, grows increasingly uncertain of his fundamental values; indeed, they undergo a major change. Reade, by contrast, remains certain of his fundamental values throughout the novel. In this, he embodies the 'considerable change' in Wilson's own outlook which Wilson says is marked by *The Glass Cage*.[24] This has important implications for *The Glass Cage* as a whole, as we shall see.

Reade lives alone in a cottage in the Lake District. He is currently working on a Blake concordance and a line-by-line commentary. He rarely reads a newspaper, has no T.V., and, when the novel opens, he has not listened to the radio for a year. He spends most of his time alone. He has never had sexual intercourse. He is, in fact, a natural ascetic, who has developed a strong mystical insight. He says:

> I try to develop . . . an ability to see the magic underneath the surface of the world. Or, to put it another way, I try to make myself into a good radio receiver, to pick up messages of purpose from the atmosphere.[25]

In Part I of the novel, which forms about a quarter of the whole, Reade's isolated rural existence is evoked. Wilson has said that in *The Glass Cage*, he was 'deliberately constructing a plot that parallels that of *Ritual*'.[26] While the parallel does not often come across strongly in *The Glass Cage*, its opening paragraph contrasts sharply with that of *Ritual*. Instead of Sorme's near-violent alienation from modern life, Reade, as he sits on a boulder in the Styhead Pass, feels 'an active sense of the benevolence of nature, a desire to become a rock pushing its shoulders into the hills'.[27] No pastoral idyll follows, however; Reade's bucolic neighbours are portrayed as stupid and inadvertently callous.

When Reade reaches home, he finds a policeman waiting. The policeman tells him about a mass murderer at large in London; he has killed six men and three women; on walls near the bodies, he leaves quotations from Blake. The policeman believes Reade may have received letters which could help in their investigations. Reade does not file all his letters, but he lets the policeman take away the drawer-full he has accumulated.

The visit leaves him feeling depressed; the modern world has broken into his isolation. He goes to see a bookseller, Urien Lewis, who lives in the nearest town. He stays the night, and the bookseller's 15-year-old ward, Sarah, joins him in bed. Reade has known her since she was 10; now he realizes she is no longer a child. She asks him to marry her, and he agrees.

In the morning, when Sarah has gone to school, Lewis offers some objections to the marriage. His main charge is that Reade is an innocent who knows nothing of the modern world. He suggests, ironically, that Reade should go to London and solve the Blake murders. Reade denies Lewis's charge; but he takes up his suggestion. For Reade, as for Sorme in *Ritual*, there must be a down-going.

We saw in Chapter Three that Wilson endorsed the idea of novels as 'thought experiments'. At this point in *The Glass Cage*, with Reade about to set off for London, we feel that we are in for a very interesting 'thought experiment': the encounter of a virginal recluse and mystic with the modern world, as represented by urban life and by a series of brutal murders. The first page of Part II brings home with naturalistic veracity the immediate impact of metropolitan life upon Reade; after that, however, his encounter with the 'great wen' becomes curiously muted. He goes to stay with a friend, Kit Butler, who lives in Notting Hill, near the Portobello Road: the setting for *Adrift in Soho*: but, in contrast to the earlier novel, this is no more than a lightly sketched backdrop. He loses his virginity with a willing young Negress called Sheila, but it is an ironic initiation, which frees him from an illusion; afterwards, 'he knew, with sudden certainty, that he would never feel any enthusiasm for the act of physical intercourse.'[28]

Detachment has always been a characteristic of Wilson's heroes, with the exception of Zweig; in Reade, it is especially evident. He is able to sink into mystical states almost at will:

> His breathing became shallow, and it seemed as if the atoms of his body were losing their energy, so that he was sinking into a state of suspended animation. A contentment that was deeper than happiness flowed over him in waves of quiet. He had a sensation as if looking down on his body, on the person called Damon Reade. The events of the past two days were present in his mind, and he found himself regarding them with a kind of tolerant gaiety. Everything seemed absurd and unimportant. . . . He saw more clearly than ever before that all his ideas about himself and the world were a misunderstanding.[29]

Reade's ability to attain mystical insights, his detachment, his certainty, mean that his encounter with the modern world is no contest; the result is a foregone conclusion. This gives *The Glass Cage* a curiously static quality, which contrasts with the sense of movement, of ambivalence, in *Necessary Doubt*. The later novel is a calm, formal demonstration. The world is *Maya*, illusion: the mystic has access to the timeless reality. *The Glass Cage* is a skilful novel of mysticism.

This means that the detective quest is less exciting than in *Necessary Doubt*, on both the thriller and existential levels. Reade's unofficial murder investigation proceeds with remarkable ease; for example, a telephone directory falls open at just the page he needs to further his enquiries. This kind of fortuitousness acts partly as a send-up of the machinery of the detective novel; but it also confirms Reade's intuitive awareness of an underlying order in the universe with which human beings, if they develop their insight sufficiently, can get in touch. Things go well for him because he is in touch with that order.

As in *Necessary Doubt*, the central quest is, of course, not criminal but existential: Reade wants to understand why a man who knows Blake is also a murderer. Like Sorme with the Whitechapel killer, Reade's feelings towards the murderer are ambivalent; he condemns killing, but cannot believe that this killer is a totally lost soul. He quotes the *Bhagavad Gita*: 'Though a man be the greatest of sinners, this knowledge will carry him like a raft above his sin.'[30] The interest of *The Glass Cage* does not lie in Reade's encounter with the modern world; that theme, effectively introduced in Part I of the novel, quickly becomes subsidiary. It lies in Reade's ambivalence towards, his urge to understand, murder. Wilson might argue that the murderer is representative of the modern world; but he does not, in the novel, convey this representative significance.

Reade's investigations quickly produce a suspect: George Gaylord Sundheim. As in *Necessary Doubt*, the hunter does not meet his quarry until the novel is well advanced; in contrast to *Necessary Doubt*, the quarry turns out to be, without any shadow of doubt, a multiple murderer. Sundheim is, once again, a larger-than-life figure. Like Caradoc Cunningham, he tends to be more a collection of attributes than a realized presence. He is physically huge; wealthy; sexually versatile. His energy is immense, but, though he is intelligent, he lacks self-discipline and a sense of purpose, so that his energy explodes in Gargantuan eating and drinking bouts, sexual orgies—and murder. He represents, like Austin Nunne, the 'futility inherent in physical life'.[31] He has a pet: a nine-foot long boa constrictor which he keeps in a glass cage.

In his relationship with Sundheim, Reade is part teacher, part psychotherapist, part prosecuting counsel. Like Sorme with Nunne, he does not feel Sundheim will turn his violence against him, and he is proved right. But Reade is not challenged by Sundheim as Sorme is by Nunne, or Zweig by Neumann. He is more like a scientist examining a specimen.

His first meeting with Sundheim convinces Reade that he cannot be the killer; he seems very gentle, uncertain, shy. Their next encounter shows him in a different light; he eats and drinks grossly, then falls asleep. Reade leaves him, but Sundheim rings him that same evening, wanting another meeting. This time when they meet, Reade gives him some of the 'no-crap therapy'

which Wilson is inclined to endorse as a form of psycho-
therapy.[32] He tells him directly: 'you're lazy and utterly
spoiled'—characteristic terms of moral condemnation for
Wilson. Sundheim tells Reade that he would like to learn
something from him, but defends himself against Reade's
criticisms, pointing out his problem with excess energy. He
then takes Reade to a dubious night club, as Nunne took Sorme
to a homosexual club-cum-brothel in *Ritual*. There is no
apotheosis of Sundheim, however, to parallel the apotheosis of
Nunne as Nijinsky; only a sordid brawl in which Sundheim
defeats two Negroes who try to rob him. Then Sundheim takes
Reade to another flat he owns; Reade spends the night on the
settee there and, when he wakes up, he finds that Sundheim has
gone. He returns to Kit Butler's, to find that Butler has called
the police, fearing that he may have been killed. He also learns
that the police now have enough evidence to arrest Sundheim.

When the police move in on Sundheim, however, he barri-
cades himself in with a revolver and starts shooting. Reade is
called in to talk to him. The siege scene has a large element of
comedy, due to Reade's detachment from it, despite the key role
that he plays. Ignoring the frantic police warnings, Reade walks
over to the flat, feeling it unlikely that Sundheim will shoot him;
he breaks down the door and starts to talk to Sundheim. As in
Ritual and *Necessary Doubt*, there is a final confrontation between
hero and hunted as the police move in. Reade persuades
Sundheim to give himself up, pointing out that the police have
no conclusive evidence that he is guilty of the murders. By the
time the police rush in, Sundheim is docile. Reade, the un-
worldly innocent, has triumphed where the worldly have failed,
because he is in touch with a reality closed to them. Knight
victorious, initiated into sex and violence, but still essentially
innocent, he can now return to marry Sarah.[34]

Despite these worldly triumphs, it is questionable whether
Reade has developed much, if at all, in the course of the novel.
His fundamental values have only been confirmed, not changed.
Sundheim, in contrast to Nunne and Neumann, is more a case-
book example than a challenge. In this, he anticipates the
murderers in Wilson's later novels, *The Killer* and *The Schoolgirl
Murder Case*. As for Reade's encounter with the modern world,
that is a non-event. In contrast to Wilson's previous novels, *The*

Glass Cage is an anti-*Bildungsroman*, in which the hero learns what he already knows.

All these features give the novel the curiously static quality we have identified. Wilson, however, is not a static mystic and he rejects the static novel; his philosophy is dynamic, evolutionary, and he wants novels that 'get somewhere'. His problem as a novelist is to express this dynamic impulse, to get somewhere, starting from the certainty he has now attained. *The Glass Cage* is a kind of high plateau, a breathing-space enjoyed after a hard climb; but Wilson sees further heights still towering above. The problem for him is how to symbolize their ascent in a novel. It is a problem he will tackle by turning next to science fiction.

NOTES

1. *Necessary Doubt* (Barker, 1964; my refs. to Village Press, 1974 ed.), p. 80.
2. *Voyage*, p. 152. For Wilson's discussion of Durrenmatt, see 'Friedrich Dürrenmatt: Heir of the Existential Tradition', Appendix Three, *Strength to Dream*, pp. 227–35.
3. *Doubt*, p. 46.
4. *Doubt*, pp. 132–33.
5. *Doubt*, p. 12.
6. *Doubt*, p. 14.
7. *Doubt*, p. 17.
8. *Doubt*, p. 18.
9. *Doubt*, pp. 166–67.
10. *Doubt*, pp. 22–3.
11. *Doubt*, p. 9.
12. *Doubt*, p. 53.
13. *Doubt*, p. 109.
14. See 'Note', *God of the Labyrinth*, p. 275.
15. *Doubt*, p. 196.
16. *Doubt*, p. 209.
17. See 'The Mescalin Experience', Appendix I, *Beyond the Outsider*, pp. 187–206.
18. *Doubt*, p. 213.
19. R. H. W. Dillard, 'Towards an Existential Realism: The Novels of Colin Wilson', *Hollins Critic*, vol. iv, no. 4 (Hollins College, Virginia, October, 1967), p. 10.
20. *Doubt*, p. 218.
21. *Doubt*, p. 233.
22. *Doubt*, p. 222.
23. *Doubt*, p. 235.

24. *Voyage*, p. 161. See also pp. 158–60.
25. *The Glass Cage* (Barker, 1966; my refs. to Village Press, n.d., ed.), p. 85.
26. *Voyage*, p. 159.
27. *Cage*, p. 3.
28. *Cage*, p. 99.
29. *Cage*, p. 100.
30. *Cage*, p. 151. *Bhagavad Gita*, 4:36. Cf. *Voyage*, p. 58.
31. See Chapter 4 above, p. 58.
32. See C. Wilson, *New Pathways in Psychology: Maslow and the Post-Freudian Revolution* (Gollancz, 1972), pp. 229, 242.
33. *Cage*, p. 166.
34. Dillard, p. 10, compares Reade going to London to 'a medieval knight [who] puts his love . . . to the test in action'.

7

Arrows to the Farther Shore: *The Mind Parasites* and *The Philosopher's Stone*

Science fiction would seem an ideal medium for Colin Wilson, since its function is the same as that of all his work: the re-definition of man in the light of the future. Science-fiction is orientated towards tomorrow; it endeavours to upset our normal, local perceptions and make us see ourselves in a cosmic context; it allows, indeed encourages, bold speculation; it is concerned with the relationships of human beings, not to each other, but to the future, the cosmos, and to non-human entities. We could call it the genre of evolution.

In Chapter One, we saw that, as a schoolboy, Wilson was a science fiction addict, and that he felt that science fiction was concerned with serious issues, as the comics and sex and violence gangster novels he had previously read were not. In 1963, before he had published any science fiction himself, Wilson elaborated his praise of the genre in *The Strength to Dream*. He claimed that it had 'escaped the general sense of defeat . . . that pervades so much modern writing' and 'often shows a vitality and inventiveness that have been absent from literature since the nineteenth-century romantics'. He argued that it could achieve 'an exciting pressure of ideas', serve as a means of trying to 'liberate the human imagination' and, at its best, sound 'an almost theological note'.[1]

The Mind Parasites (1967) and *The Philosopher's Stone* (1969) are both science-fiction novels, and they are closely linked in theme and style. Indeed, *The Mind Parasites* could be seen as a prelude to its much longer successor. It must be stressed at the outset that both novels, especially the later, intrigue on a first or second reading; they succeed as popular science fiction, but they also promise more; this is why we return to them. We then ask if they fulfil their promise.

Both novels are first-person accounts by men who, during the course of their narratives, make the 'evolutionary leap'. As Gilbert Austin says in *The Mind Parasites*: 'At last we understood clearly Teilhard de Chardin's remark that man stands on the brink of a new phase in his evolution. For we were now *in* that new phase.'[2] At the end of *Necessary Doubt*, we saw Zweig and Neumann standing on that brink. In *The Glass Cage*, we found a man who had reached a high plateau of certainty but who, despite evolutionary gestures, remained essentially static. In these two novels, we go over the brink; we take imaginary voyages into the evolutionary beyond.

Both novels make much play with the private mythology created by the American writer, H. P. Lovecraft (1890–1937). Lovecraft was a recluse who lived in Providence, Rhode Island. He was an eccentric with a fierce hatred of the modern world. He wrote stories for 'pulp' magazines such as *Weird Tales*, *Amazing Stories* and *Astounding Science Fiction*; at first these were stories of horror, fantasy and the supernatural, but they moved towards science fiction, and Lovecraft began to develop in them a mythology which was, in his own words, 'based on the fundamental lore or legend that this world was inhabited at one time by another race, who, in practising black magic, lost their foothold and were expelled, yet live on outside ever ready to take possession of the earth again.'[3]

Wilson claims to have first discovered Lovecraft in 1959.[4] But *Amazing Stories*, to which Lovecraft contributed, was one of the science-fiction magazines Wilson collected as a schoolboy; it seems possible that he may have read Lovecraft in some back numbers, even if he does not consciously recall this. In his first published critique of Lovecraft, in *The Strength to Dream*, Wilson expressed interest in Lovecraft's rejection of the everyday world and his view of life as dark, strange and extraordinary, and affirmed that Lovecraft stood in 'a recognizable romantic tradition'. Nonetheless, he is 'a very bad writer'.[5] This provoked a response from the American science fiction writer, the late August Derleth; Derleth protested at Wilson's low estimate of Lovecraft and challenged him to write a Lovecraftian novel himself. *The Mind Parasites* and *The Philosopher's Stone* are, in part, a response to this challenge, and they show Wilson's deepening interest in Lovecraft. Wilson seems to regard him with a mixture of identification and rejection. He has acknowledged that, in his mid-teens, he greatly resembled Lovecraft; he felt 'the same pessimism, the same world-contempt, the same hatred of everything modern'.[6] Lovecraft's embattled stance, his 'Outsiderism', also appeal to him; recently, he has stated: 'I have nothing but admiration for Lovecraft's magnificent intransigence in the face of a world he found futile and destructive.'[7] But Wilson has affirmed that he no longer shares Lovecraft's pessimism and world-hatred.

The presence of Lovecraftian elements in *The Mind Parasites* and *The Philosopher's Stone* should not, however, blind us to their essential concern with evolutionary existentialism. As they are both first-person accounts, they give wide scope to Wilson's didacticism and could, indeed, serve as a summary of all his major ideas. Man has enormous hidden powers; he does not make use of them due to laziness and blindness. If he could learn to release them at will, he would have made the leap into the next phase of evolution; he would have immensely enhanced powers of perception and intellection; he would develop powers that are now seen as 'occult' or non-existent, such as telepathy and psychokinesis; he would have no need of other people, though he would be able to establish instant telepathic contact with them; he would be able to live almost wholly in the 'world of the mind', despite a continued basic dependence on matter; he would be free of disease (both novels make much of the idea that cancer is a psychosomatic disease, caused by frustration) and his lifespan would be greatly extended.

In his 'Preface' to *Man Without A Shadow*, Wilson defined what he saw as a key possibility for the novel:

> This consists in trying to tell a story, but to raise the story to the level of reality. One might say that the ideal story for this type of

novel would be the life story of a saint who finally achieves 'transcendent reality'. If the novelist could describe this reality in such a way that the reader was transported into it, this would be the ideally great novel, for it would move on the level of a story, yet end by bringing the reader to 'reality'.[8]

In Wilson's terms, the story of a man who has made the 'evolutionary leap' is even more suitable for such a novel than a saint's life-story. Saintliness involves, beyond a certain point of willed self-discipline, humility, dependence on a higher power, prayer, submission, surrender of the will; these are alien to a dynamic, self-actualizing evolutionary drive. The heroes of *The Mind Parasites* and *The Philosopher's Stone* have discovered their *own* power and strength of will. Their stories provide Wilson with a great opportunity. If he can achieve a sufficiently rich vision of the 'evolutionary leap', he will have made a decisive contribution, the most important yet, to the literature of evolutionary existentialism.

Wilson's higher men, however, sound suspiciously like their unelevated author. To some extent, of course, this is inevitable; to write like a higher man, it would be necessary to be a higher man, and one of Wilson's major points is that such men do not yet exist. This apparent failure to render the consciousness of higher men could be seen as an alienation effect which directs our attention away from the fantasy to the ideas and reminds us that the task of evolving into higher men still lies before us, as Brecht wished to remind his audience that they still had to achieve a free and just society. This argument has some validity. But such an alienation effect, in directing our attention to the ideas, makes us examine those ideas more critically. A number of points emerge from this examination.

First, the ideas seem insufficiently complex. We do not have the sense of a mind grappling with the difficulties that a respect for minute particulars discloses. We might think that one of the characteristics of a higher man would be an ability to assimilate a far wider range of data than is possible for unelevated minds. Although the narrators of these two novels tell us they can do this—Austin, for example, says that 'without the slightest effort, I grasped the theory of functions, multi-dimensional geometry, quantum mechanics, game theory and group theory'[9]—the operations of their minds, as conveyed to us by

Wilson's prose, do not support their claims. Both, of course, blame this on the inadequacy of the all-too-human language they have to use; and we would not expect a science fiction novel to be a philosophical treatise; but it would help if we could sense a greater pressure of mind behind the inevitably simplified language. Wilson's higher men, in fact, seem to be filtering out much of the data that contributes to our present level of complexity; to be simplifying, not enriching, reality. Wilson does communicate, however, feelings of excitement and euphoria, often of a narcissistic kind; this is why these novels tend to work well on a first or second reading, but less so subsequently.

The most important aspect of this lack of complexity in these novels is their tendency, both in the attitudes the narrators express, and in the events that occur, to soar too far above the human and physical world. Science fiction is a mode which allows, in fact encourages, moving away from our normal conceptions of reality, away from the human and physical world; but the further away a specific novel does move, the more difficult it is to give it structure and significance, since our sense of structure and significance is closely bound up with the human and physical world. Wilson's case is that the deepest structures and significances come from outside that world— from a 'Life Force', as Shaw would have called it, from God in traditional Christian terms—and this is a perfectly coherent view. The fact is, however, that we express our sense of structures and significances in a language which is grounded in the human and physical world; this means that it is very difficult to convey convincingly, in a novel, the sense of a source of values that is largely independent of that world, especially in view of the novel's close links with empirical reality. It is even more difficult if that world is persistently denigrate in a novel. But in *The Mind Parasites* and *The Philosopher's Stone* Wilson, in this respect a true disciple of Lovecraft, does just this. In discussing each novel individually, we shall focus on this rejection of the human and physical world and the difficulties that ensue; it is the feature of both novels that emerges most strongly upon re-reading and it points to a weakness in the evolutionary existentialist philosophy.

Wilson traces the seed of *The Mind Parasites* to an analogy he uses in *Introduction to the New Existentialism* (1966):

> it would seem that there is some mysterious agency that wishes to hold men back, to prevent them from gaining full use of their powers. It is as if man contained an invisible parasite, whose job it is to keep man unaware of his freedom.[10]

The narrative of the novel purports to be made up from tape-recordings and writings by Professor Gilbert Austin. It begins in 1994 and details Austin's discovery of the mind parasites, who have been at work on the human mind since the Romantic period; describes his battle against them, helped by a few select comrades; and concludes with an editorial note on Austin's mysterious disappearance from a spaceship in 2007. The parasites provide Wilson with an engaging symbol of the problem which preoccupies him—the fickleness of human consciousness, the failure of human will—and the story of the battle against them, enlivened by Lovecraftian detail, passes the time well enough. The main serious point of the novel, however, is that Austin, by fighting the parasites, is able to achieve his evolutionary breakthrough by means of will-power; he can (so he tells us) think faster, enter the 'world of the mind' whenever he wants to and call upon paranormal powers such as telepathy and psychokinesis.

It is his new-found powers which justify his contempt for the human and physical world—especially for its human aspect. We have traced in Wilson's previous novels, *Necessary Doubt* excepted, an increasing tendency to detachment on the part of the heroes. This reached a peak with Damon Reade in *The Glass Cage*, but it was mitigated by his gentleness. In Gilbert Austin and his colleagues, it appears in a much harsher light, partly because it is, on their own valuation, largely justified:

> As we crossed the main square . . . we found ourselves looking at these people around us with a kind of god-like pity. They were all so preoccupied with their petty worries, all enmeshed in their personal little daydreams, while we at last were grappling with *reality*—the only true reality, that of the evolution of mind.[11]

This is akin to Uncle Sam's vision of humanity in *The World of Violence*. It is true that Austin and his allies show a heightened awareness of the beauty of the physical world, but this only seems to make the human world more intolerable. For example, when they return to earth from a trip to the moon:

> Everything seemed infinitely more beautiful than we had remembered it. . . . On the other hand, the human beings who greeted us seemed alien and repulsive, little better than apes. It was suddenly incredible that these morons could inhabit this infinitely beautiful world and yet remain so blind and stupid.[12]

Certainly such passages suggest that Wilson has absorbed the attitudes of Lovecraft; but he has said that he wrote his Lovecraftian novels as a means of criticizing Lovecraft[13]; at moments like these, he seems to identify with Lovecraft too completely. Furthermore, such outbursts seem rather beneath a higher man. In this half of the twentieth century, we have developed a certain ecological consciousness, have begun to learn to respect animals and the environment. Wilson's higher men seem to lack this consciousness; they see men as animals, but do not respect them. Austin makes a few condescending gestures towards love for mankind; for example, shortly after the above outburst, he reflects that these 'creatures might be little more than idiots, yet they were still brothers'—but his basic attitude is clear.[14] Most men are apes; only 'a small percentage of the human race . . . are evolutionary animals with a deep and powerful urge to become truly free.'[15] Austin, in this like Wilson himself, promotes an evolutionary Calvinism, in which only an elect can be saved.

Now this contempt for the bulk of humanity, while it may have religious precedents, stands condemned by Wilson's own criteria. First, it often seems to be a 'human, all-too-human' expression of irritation and impatience—petty personal emotions. Secondly, it commits what is, for Wilson, the cardinal sin: it devalues life, by making humanity seem much less interesting, courageous, ingenious, enduring, than history and anthropology, for all the evidence of weakness, stupidity and brutality that they also provide, suggest it to be. Wilson has accused certain writers, as we saw in Chapter Three, of libelling life, of presenting a partial view of it as if it were a total one; Graham Greene, for instance. Austin's attitude to the human race, however, which Wilson endorses, is itself a slander, a partial distorted view. A total view of humanity would incorporate both negative and positive features; Austin holds the unbalanced view of a misanthrope; the view of Lovecraft himself.

With this devaluation of the human race goes, not surprisingly, a devaluation of human society:

> [The] 'secret life' inside . . . is the reality; other people are mere shadows in comparison. . . . [For] the 'shadows' . . . human society is the reality. They are entirely concerned with its personal little values, with its pettiness and malice and self-seeking.[16]

Once more, we can turn Wilson's own criteria against him and point out that he is libelling life, presenting a part as the whole. This completely negative attitude to society is romantic world-rejection at its most callow. Wilson would claim that, by the time he came to write *The Mind Parasites*, he had gone 'beyond the Outsider', but this is rank Outsiderism. A true higher man would, we feel, recognize the limitations and failures of human society throughout the centuries, but would also acknowledge its considerable achievements, which include the art, literature, philosophy and science of mankind—which would not have been possible without society. This is not sentimental humanism, but sound anthropology. Austin's attitude to *homo sapiens* reminds us of the unjustly contemptuous attitude that *homo sapiens* once held towards Neanderthal man.

Austin's attitude to the human world does show some ambivalence. We may recall that at the end of *Necessary Doubt*, as Zweig stood on the edge of the evolutionary breakthrough, 'the life in him squirmed away from some realization, as from a cold wind.' In *The Mind Parasites*, with the evolutionary breakthrough made, we understand the nature of that realization: that the evolutionary leap will separate him from the human world. This is emphasized by the feelings of Austin and his companions as they go out into space:

> as we separated from the rest of humankind, our first sensation was a terrible fear and loneliness, like a child being separated from its mother for the first time.[17]

They quickly overcome this, however, by 'a new turning-inward, to the "source of power, meaning and purpose".' It is the contact of each individual with 'the power-house' that saves him from total isolation, from solipsism. Austin says:

> man is never 'alone', for he is directly connected to the universal powerhouse. . . . You could be the last man alive in the universe, and you would not be alone.[18]

This is the final justification of the higher man's contempt for humanity. This passage shows clearly that Wilson, like earlier proponents of Creative Evolution, is trying to find a replacement for words like 'God'.

Austin's attitude to human beings and human society has two consequences for the success of *The Mind Parasites* as a novel. On the level of plot, it means that the excitement, the sense of risk, is muted; saving the human race from the parasites does not matter too much, if the bulk of it is hardly worth saving anyway. This is made explicit by one of Austin's fellow-supermen:

> It's funny. I ought to be thinking about the danger that confronts the human race. . . . Instead . . . I feel a kind of contempt for these people wandering by in the street. They're all asleep. It doesn't really seem to matter much what happens to them. . . .[19]

We can trace in Wilson's novels so far, as a corollary to the growing detachment of the hero, an increasing sense that 'it doesn't really seem to matter much what happens'. (*Necessary Doubt* is, once again, an exception.) In *The Glass Cage*, this leads to stasis: nothing really happens. *The Mind Parasites* tries to make things happen again, but they do not seem significant; a strong feeling pervades the novel that 'it doesn't really seem to matter much what happens', except on some exalted, ethereal plane. As far as the human world is concerned, this feeling comes close to nihilism at times.

The loss of significance produced by the devaluation of human beings and human society also vitiates the novel on its more serious level, that of evolutionary parable. It means, furthermore, that important and interesting implications—that is, imaginative possibilities—are not confronted and developed. What of the non-evolutionary nineteen-twentieths of humanity? Wilson offers some hints: for example, Austin and his colleagues are instrumental in bringing about the establishment of a 'Unified World Government' and they select intelligent teenagers and children for special training. But these are not followed up; Austin disappears into the empyrean. What kind of society is going to emerge? A Brave New World, a totalitarian dystopia, seems all too likely. Might not an Ivan Karamazov of this future feel that he wants to hand back his entrance ticket to the evolutionary spearhead? Wilson seems to feel that, once the evolutionary breakthrough that he foresees is made, all social and political problems on the human plane will be solved. In view of the contempt for common humanity which is built into his profile of the New Man, this seems unlikely; and the ethical issues would be enormous.

By assuming that all such problems will be easily solved and by making Austin and his comrades completely independent of humanity, Wilson brings his novel to an end: what is there to write about? What, indeed, is the point of writing, if one is, like Gilbert Austin, sufficient to oneself alone, freed from the need to communicate, seeing most of one's likely audience as little better than apes? What is the point of doing anything? Inevitably Austin and friends soar into the beyond. In a sense, their universe is very simple; it lacks complexity and, with the parasites conquered, it lacks negativity; without negativity, it lacks limits and therefore lacks structure. Evolution is complexification, according to Teilhard de Chardin's maxim; with Austin, it is simplification: an evasion, not a mastering, of problems. This vision of the future is too Lovecraftian: too much like the wish-fulfilment fantasy of a solipsistically inclined recluse.

The Philosopher's Stone is a much more substantial and, in some ways, more satisfactory novel. In Part I, Howard Lester gives an account of his early life and the events leading up to his evolutionary breakthrough. This is the most successful section of the book; it could stand alone as a self-contained short novel. But then it is the prelude to the 'evolutionary leap'; it aims less high than what follows.

Part I is a blend of *Bildungsroman*, scientific detective story (James D. Watson's *Double Helix* would be a factual analogy), philosophical treatise and science fiction tale. It focuses on the problem of death.

The *Bildungsroman* bears some resemblance to the early chapters of *The World of Violence*. Howard, like Hugh Greene, is a precocious, highly intelligent boy. Hugh's early awareness of violence matches Howard's early awareness of death:

> I had borrowed a book on early music from the library. That cold, modal music of the Middle Ages continued to exert its strange attraction over me. In the chapter on ancient Greek music, I discovered the Skolion of Seikilos, with its words:
>
> > May life's sun upon thee smile
> > Far from pain and sorrow.
> > Life is far too short, alas.
> > Death the kraken waits to drown you
> > In the sea of earth.
>
> . . . The lines made me feel cold. All the same, I went up to our attic and tried out the skolion on our old piano, picking out the Phrygian scale, then playing it through until I understood the shape of the melody. Again, the coldness settled on me, and I murmured the words aloud as I played, feeling the same immense sadness, the sensation of infinite distances, that I had experienced in the churchyard. Suddenly, my mind said: What are you doing, you fool? This is *real*, not a literary metaphor. There is not a person alive in the world today who will still be alive in a hundred years from now. . . . And I grasped the reality, the truth of my own death. The horror almost choked me. I felt too weak to keep my hands on the keyboard, too weak to sit on the piano stool without support.[20]

At the age of 13, Howard meets Sir Alastair Lyell, a wealthy scientist. Despite their difference in age and social status, they instantly become friends. Lyell, besides his scientific interests, is a man of wide general culture. He unofficially adopts Howard; Howard goes to live at his large country house, and there they pursue a 'life of the mind', devoted to study, scientific research and cultural pursuits. In *The World of Violence*, Hugh was fortunate, as a child, to meet exceptional adults, Nick and Sam; the 13-year-old Howard is even more fortunate in meeting Lyell. He comments:

> At thirteen, my mind was hungry; I could feel myself changing almost daily. Without Lyell, it would have been a period of

107

frustration—of increasing desire to live a life of 'sensations and ideas', and hatred of the everyday world that prevented this. . . . What Lyell offered me was not abnormal intellectual activity, but a life of discovery and purpose. Thirteen is the age of what Shaw calls 'the birth of the moral passion'—that is, the period when ideas are not abstractions but realities, when they are food and drink. The changes of puberty have altered one's old conception of oneself. Identity vanishes; one's inner being becomes formless, chaos waiting for the act of creation. There is a brooding feeling of anticipation; the clouds lie there, fragmentary, slate grey, waiting for the wind. And a book, a symphony, a poem, is not merely another 'experience' but a mystery, a wind blowing from the future. The problem of death is still far away; but the problem of life seems quite as tremendous. The mind contemplates vistas of time, the emptiness of space, and knows that the 'ordinariness' of everyday life is an illusion. And as the everyday becomes less real, so ideas are seen to be the only reality, and the mind that shapes them the only true power in this world of blind natural forces.[21]

The world of discovery, purpose and ordered development that Howard finds with Lyell is very different from the world of Wilson's own teens, and we feel that we are reading a wish-fulfilment fantasy, yet one that is curiously convincing because it springs from deep promptings in its author's experience. In *The World of Violence*, Wilson conveyed the intellectual awakening that a child can experience; in *The Philosopher's Stone*, he does the same with a teenager. Despite the considerable attention given to teenage psychology in recent years, this area remains comparatively neglected.

Behind Lyell's ordered world, however, death stands waiting. For Howard, as for Hugh Greene, there are two worlds, order and chaos. While he is with Lyell, chaos is kept at bay. He occasionally talks about death with Lyell, but Lyell shows no interest. Then, suddenly, Lyell dies:

[It] came as the greatest shock I had ever experienced. . . .

I somehow took it for granted that Lyell would live to be a centenarian and that I would attend his funeral in Westminster Abbey. . . . His death at fifty-seven seemed so murderously stupid that my sense of 'rightness' was shaken. I felt a cold suspicion that I had been living an illusion for the past twelve years.[22]

Howard decides that death is the most important of all problems and sets out on his researches into gerontology. This confrontation with death, a universal human concern, gives Part I of *The Philosopher's Stone* its urgency and significance.

In his 'Prefatory Note' to the novel, Wilson explicitly acknowledges that he is following the example of Shaw in *Back to Methuselah* and trying to write a 'parable of longevity'.[23] Shaw said that, in *Back to Methuselah*, he was exploiting 'the eternal interest of the philosopher's stone which enables men to live for ever' and Wilson could say the same of this novel; Shaw's remark is clearly the source of its title.[24] Howard comes to endorse Shaw's view, which Wilson also shares, that we die of 'laziness and want of conviction and failure to make our lives worth living'.[25] In other words, death is a moral failing; Howard, like his creator, is an evolutionary moralist.

There is an important difference, however, between the attitudes to longevity of Shaw and Wilson. For Shaw, longer life produces greater consciousness; for Wilson, greater consciousness yields longer life. This gets Wilson round the difficulty raised by Swift, in his depiction of the Struldbrugs, and by Aldous Huxley in *After Many A Summer*: that longer life may lead, not to development, but to degeneration.

Once he begins his researches into death, Howard, though he does not yet fully realize it, is on an evolutionary quest: for the answer to death is enlarged consciousness, and enlarged consciousness is the key to the next phase in human evolution.

At first, he can find no scientific verification for his theory that people die because they lose the will to live. Sometimes, he feels that he is dangerously close to becoming a crank. Then he makes contact with another scientist, Sir Henry Littleway, who is concerned with man's evolutionary development. Littleway introduces him to the work of Aaron Marks, a psychologist who has researched into 'value experiences'. Marks's ideas are clearly those of Abraham Maslow, and his 'value experiences' are Maslow's 'peak experiences'. Howard becomes convinced that the rate of human ageing would be arrested, or greatly slowed, if people could enjoy a constant supply of 'value experiences'.

He and Littleway are given the chance to experiment on a farm labourer whose brain has been pierced by the spike of a combine harvester, and who has since been in a virtually permanent state of childlike ecstasy; he is 'a Wordsworth without the power of self-expression, a Traherne who could only say "Gor, ain't it pretty"'.[26] As he can permanently enjoy 'value experiences' he should, if Howard's theory is correct, age far more slowly, if at all. But he dies of a brain tumour.

With his theory shattered, Howard plunges into a severe depression; he soon revives, however, with the realization that 'value experiences' in themselves will not prolong life. The answer is to increase the ability of human consciousness to perceive a far wider network of relationships, to attain a state of 'contemplative objectivity'. It is never made quite clear why this should necessarily produce longer life; but Howard states that 'it is so'.[27] Howard and Littleway turn their attention to brain physiology to try and find ways to attain greater 'relational consciousness'. After two years, they discover that a special alloy, when inserted in minute quantities into the brain's prefrontal cortex, produces a state of wide 'relational consciousness', of 'contemplative objectivity'. The alloy was developed by an Alois Neumann, who had a son called Gustav: echoes of *Necessary Doubt*. After experimenting on two other people, Howard tries the Neumann alloy himself. It works. The evolutionary breakthrough has been made, symbolized, as in *Necessary Doubt*, by a science fiction device.

In Part II of the novel, Howard quickly discovers that he can sustain intense 'relational consciousness' by will-power alone. He asserts that the problem of human ageing has now been solved. Littleway soon follows Howard in taking the 'evolutionary leap'.

With two higher men on his hands, and a lot of the novel still to go, Wilson tries to show them in action. He runs into difficulties, however. As in *The Mind Parasites*, the consciousnesses rendered do not seem much like those of higher men. In the earlier novel, however, the battle against the parasites acted as a structuring device; at this stage in *The Philosopher's Stone*, structure is lacking. Howard enjoys a virtually permanent state of 'holiday consciousness' and, as on most holidays that go on too long, he seems uncertain of what to do with himself. The novel turns into a compendium of games. Howard uses his powers to find further evidence that Bacon wrote Shakespeare's plays (in the process concluding that the plays consist of 'fine language with totally trivial content');[28] drives away a poltergeist that is troubling a suburban family called Mudd; learns how to project images from his mind into the external world; and develops a power of 'time-vision' which enables him to see into the past. He even manages, almost by the way, to get married to a willing and self-effacing woman. Although he frequently affirms his vitality, will-power and sense of purpose, with an enthusiasm worthy of Norman Vincent Peale, his activities seem frivolous rather than purposive, trivial rather than serious.

The Old Ones seem to be introduced into the novel in an attempt to re-establish a sense of direction and seriousness, to bring in the structural support which the battle against the mind parasites gave to the previous novel. The Old Ones are borrowed from Lovecraft's work. They are vast mental beings who originally created men in order to serve them, by arresting the embryonic development of apes. Under the Old Ones, the great legendary civilization of Mu was established, a kind of totalitarian dystopia dominated by a priest-caste who were in direct contact with the Old Ones. But the Old Ones found that men were evolving faster than them, and they decided that they must take on some human characteristics; develop bodies, for example. But this demanded an enormous amount of conscious effort and self-discipline, which led them to suppress and try to ignore the less conscious levels of their being; in the end, the unacknowledged energies at these levels took revenge, bursting out to wreak large-scale havoc. Unable to control the energies, the Old Ones decided to use them to make themselves unconscious for an indefinite period, millions of years on the human time-scale. Since then, man has been left to evolve on his own, although the priest-caste continued to exist for many thousands of years before dying out. One day, however, perhaps soon, the Old Ones will awaken again.

Once Howard and Littleway discover the existence of the Old Ones, they enter into battle with them, and this takes up the last part of the novel. They also delve deeply into the history of the Old Ones, mainly by means of their power of 'time-vision'. The threat the Old Ones pose reinforces the evolutionary imperative for man. It is a race against time.

The Old Ones do not revive the novel, however. The description of K'tholo (Lovecraft's Cthulhu), the high priest of Mu, who bears some likeness to Dostoevsky's Grand Inquisitor, has a certain power; but the main effect of the Old Ones is to turn *The Philosopher's Stone* into a glorified adventure tale. They cannot give the sense of urgency which the idea of death brought to Part I of the novel. Death has the weight of an existential reality; the Old Ones are fantasy. That fantasy has the kind of interest which eccentric speculations about the origins of mankind can hold, but this disappears after several readings, and the fantasy seems essentially trivial—unreal, compared to the reality of death. The sense of significance that comes from facing central issues is lost. At the end of the novel, it is death, not the Old Ones, who still waits. The theme of death gives urgency and centrality to Part I of the novel but also provides a standard which measures the limitations of the optimistic projection of Part II. The Old Ones seem like an attempt to bring back to Part II the sense of danger, risk and crisis which has disappeared with the disappearance of death. But it is unsuccessful.

This is not to say that the 'thought experiment' of the consequences of men achieving the evolutionary leap and post-poning death indefinitely is invalid. It is rather that, in this novel, we do not feel that the consequences have been adequately envisaged.

An important reason for this sense of inadequacy is that Howard, like Gilbert Austin, rejects the human and physical world. He does not give vent to irritable contempt for other people as frequently as Austin. He can even, when he wants to, achieve an intense, telepathic awareness of another person. For example, he intuits the 'feminine essence' of a girl of whom he had previously thought little, and this leads into a vision of universal love and sympathy, in which he feels that 'Jesus had been a visionary of the most incredible order'.[29] He hints, however, that this may have been part of a campaign by the Old Ones to lull him into a false sense of security, and overall, his basic attitude to humanity is close to Austin's. He shows even less interest in social and political organization than Austin, although he airily acknowledges that he 'may end as the world leader of these childish creatures called human beings'.[30] Like

Austin's, Howard's view of the human world can be seen, by Wilson's own criteria, as reductionist, devaluing, a libel. Furthermore, it weakens the novel by excluding a major field of imaginative possibility.

The grounds of Howard's world-rejection are more clearly laid-out than Austin's, however. Howard is a dualist. He cites T. E. Hulme's view that 'life'—by which he seems to mean something very much like 'mind' or 'spirit'—'has invaded the realm of matter' and that 'life' and matter are at war. This war is evolution: evolution is the increasing control of 'life' over matter: and in man this control is synonymous with an increasing ability to inhabit the 'world of the mind'. In a 'time-vision' of an Elizabethan street, Howard calls himself 'purely an observing mind', and becoming a pure, observing mind sometimes seems to be the ultimate aim of his evolutionary development.[32] Howard does assert a continued basic dependence on the body and the physical world; to escape from matter is death; but activity in the world shared with others, in the human world of man in relationship to matter, which has played an extremely important part in man's evolution to date, is no longer really necessary.

The enlarged states of mind, of 'relational consciousness', that Howard enjoys as a result of his evolutionary breakthrough, do incorporate intense experiences of 'other-ness': of a sense of the reality of other times and places, the Faculty X experience. But such experiences leave out the otherness of the physical world, and the otherness of other people as bodies in that world, as it is experienced through our senses. Howard does sometimes enjoy heightened perceptions of the immediate physical environment, and, as we have seen, heightened 'intuitions' of other people, but he regards these as much less important than the experiences of otherness that he enjoys without immediate sensory stimuli. This devalues a vast range of human experience, and suggests the idealism lying beneath Wilson's existentialism. It is a devaluation as extreme, in its way, as the behaviourist devaluation of inner experience which Wilson denounces. Such a devaluation undermines Wilson's claim, in his 'Prefatory Note' to the novel, that his idea of 'time-vision' solves the problem of presenting a plausible version of 'time-travel'.[33] This 'solution' is only arrived at by omitting one of the most compelling aspects of the notion of time-travel: the idea of being present in the body in the past and thus in physical, sensuous contact with the past. Howard, in his time-visions, is 'purely an observing mind'. Wilson's disembodied time-travel is impoverished time-travel.

Howard's devaluation of the human and physical world represents an impoverishment in Wilson's whole image of evolved man, and thus a weakening of the whole novel. It results in a loss of a sense of reality, of responsibility, of those values and significances which are articulated in and by the shared human world, even if their ultimate source lies outside that world. Howard, and the novel, become unbalanced. Once, Howard considers this:

> I got an uncomfortable feeling that I had gone too far, that I was upsetting the 'balance of nature' by this development of 'head power'. Then I realized that I was the victim of muddled thinking. There is no balance of nature. Nature is a tug of war, and I was winning it.[34]

The matter is not so easily settled, however; we feel that Wilson could have gone more deeply into it. It is bound to strike the reader that there is a certain unacknowledged parallel between Howard's development and that of the Old Ones. The Old Ones came close to destroying themselves by evolving too fast. Howard tells us:

> They had overlooked one absurd point. As the conscious mind learnt to project its visions of reason and order, the vast energies of the subconscious writhed in their prison, and projected visions of chaos.[35]

It seems, then, that 'Nature' has a way of taking revenge if it is ignored. Howard, of course, claims that he has far greater control over 'the vast energies of the subconscious' than the Old Ones; but he seems to show distinct signs of *hubris*. The claims of 'Nature'—of the human and physical world—are not so easily disposed of: they haunt *The Philosopher's Stone* and can make its optimism seem hollow, unreal.

This leads us to the basic weakness of both Wilson's science fiction novels. Science fiction gives the writer a licence to speculate freely; but not too freely. Wilson 'allows such a variety of magical events that his fictional world seems deficient in its own natural laws'.[36] The claims of the human and physical world are denied too completely, and Wilson cannot find an adequate alternative world to give a sense of resistance and difficulty, of structure and reality. Thus these novels come too close to displaying the kind of 'arbitrary and whimsical development' that we associate with fantasy rather than science fiction.[37] Anything is possible, so nothing happens. As an attempt to create a myth of evolutionary man, they come close to what the science fiction writer Olaf Stapledon called 'false myth':

> A false myth is one which either violently transgresses the limits of credibility set by its own cultural matrix, or expresses admirations less developed than those of its culture's best vision.[38]

The myths in *The Mind Parasites* and *The Philosopher's Stone* fail to show a proper respect for the limits of credibility, and, in their devaluation of the human and physical world in which the 'best vision' of our culture recognizes sources, though not necessarily the only sources, of value and significance, they express reduced admirations.

NOTES

1. *Strength to Dream*, pp. 117, 120, 121, 122, 124.
2. *Mind Parasites*, pp. 135–36.
3. Quoted in August Derleth, 'An Introduction to H. P. Lovecraft', *The Haunter of the Dark and other Tales of Terror* (Panther, 1972), pp. 8–9.
4. C. Wilson, 'Introduction', George Hay ed., *The Necronomicon* (Spearman, 1978; my ref. to Corgi, 1978 ed.), p. 17.
5. *Strength to Dream*, pp. 32, 30.
6. *Voyage*, p. 47.
7. 'Introduction', *Necronomicon*, p. 19.
8. 'Preface', *Man Without A Shadow*, p. 10.
9. *Parasites*, p. 93.
10. *Intro to New Existm*, p. 161. 'Prefatory Note', *Philosopher's Stone*, p. 6.
11. *Parasites*, p. 77.
12. *Parasites*, p. 199.
13. 'Introduction', *Necronomicon*, p. 19.
14. *Parasites*, p. 199.
15. *Parasites*, p. 180.

16. *Parasites*, p. 191.
17. *Parasites*, p. 192.
18. *Parasites*, pp. 191–92.
19. *Parasites*, p. 155.
20. *Philosopher's Stone*, p. 11.
21. *Stone*, p. 19.
22. *Stone*, pp. 22–4.
23. 'Prefatory Note', *Stone*, p. 5.
24. 'Preface', *Back to Methuselah*, p. 62.
25. Quoted in C. Wilson, *Origins of the Sexual Impulse* (Barker, 1963), p. 180. Cf. *Stone*, p. 100.
26. *Stone*, p. 66.
27. *Stone*, p. 100.
28. *Stone*, p. 131.
29. *Stone*, pp. 200–1.
30. *Stone*, p. 103.
31. *Stone*, p. 147.
32. *Stone*, p. 139.
33. 'Prefatory Note', *Stone*, pp. 6–7.
34. *Stone*, p. 147.
35. *Stone*, p. 263.
36. Robert Scholes, *Structural Fabulation: An Essay on Fiction of the Future* (University of Notre Dame Press, 1975), p. 43.
37. Kingsley Amis, *New Maps of Hell: A Survey of Science Fiction* (Gollancz, 1961), p. 23.
38. Quoted in *Structural Fabulation*, p. 21. From Stapledon's 'Preface' to his novel *Last and First Men*.

8

Murder, Sex and Spying: *The Killer*, *The God of the Labyrinth*, *The Black Room*

After the extravagant fantasy of *The Mind Parasites* and *The Philosopher's Stone*, we move in *The Killer* (1970) to the other extreme of quasi-documentary. In his 'Introduction' to this work, Wilson explains his intention of writing a 'genuine non-fiction novel' which, like Karl Berg's *The Sadist*, a study of the real-life mass murderer Peter Kürten, should be 'as compelling as a novel' but have 'a clinical realism which gives it a brutal impact far beyond the range of fiction'. For his study of a killer, however, Wilson does not take a single real-life example but builds a composite figure out of features drawn from several actual murderers. Wilson says that if it was pointed out that *The Killer* read 'more like a shilling shocker than a non-fiction novel', he would not dispute this; he asserts that 'the two are not incompatible'.[1]

The novel consists of a first-person narrative by Samuel Kahn, a prison psychiatrist. It is a kind of informal psychiatric casebook. Working at an open prison, Kahn meets Arthur Lingard, who is serving an eight-year sentence for manslaughter. After helping Lingard to emerge from a catatonic state, Kahn becomes fascinated by him and investigates the sources of his criminality in his childhood and adolescence. He eventually

117

discovers that Lingard is a multiple sex killer. Shortly afterwards, Lingard is transferred to Broadmoor, and murdered by
another prisoner there.

Under the *persona* of Kahn, Wilson is very sparing in discussing his ideas, in contrast to his didacticism in *The Mind
Parasites* and *The Philosopher's Stone*. The emphasis, as in Berg's
Sadist, is on the 'facts'. But the documentary aspect of *The Killer*,
which is so important to it, is unsuccessful for a number of
reasons.

First of all, the 'facts' are highly unpleasant. While this might
have some justification (though how much is questionable) in a
study of a real-life murderer, it seems gratuitous here. Secondly,
Wilson's whole idea of giving *The Killer* the impact of fact is
invalidated because we know that it is not fact: we treat it quite
differently. Perhaps Wilson's accumulation of detail is, in part,
an attempt to compensate for this, as if enough fictional facts
could acquire true factual status. The details are not fully
assimilated into a whole, however; no doubt this is partly due to
the variety of sources from which Wilson drew them. The novel
is overloaded and loses the structured, selective impact that
fiction can have. *The Killer* forfeits the advantages of both fact
and fiction, losing the authority of the one and the form of the
other.

The bias towards documentary, and the nature of the
supposed facts which are documented, limit the range of the
novel. In his 'Introduction', Wilson says that *The Killer* should
be seen, with *Ritual in the Dark* and *The Glass Cage*, as the third of
a criminal trilogy.[2] In the two earlier novels however, as well as
in *The World of Violence*, the themes of murder and sexual
deviance were assimilated into a larger whole; the positive
development (or, in Damon Reade's case, positive nature) of
the hero counteracted the negative degeneration of the murderer, and the hero had many experiences to balance his
encounters with violence, sexual deviance and death. Thus
these novels have an optimistic, spacious air, despite the unpleasantness of some of their themes. In *The Killer*, Kahn,
though well balanced enough, is essentially the reporter, not
the hero. Lingard, who is the centre of the book, has some
positive moments, but is, inevitably, a largely negative character. Uncharacteristically for a Wilson novel, the atmosphere of

118

The Killer is oppressive and claustrophobic. This is a failing in Wilson's own terms: he attacks novelists who emphasize violence and futility because they give a distorted image of existence: but *The Killer*, because of its documentary focus on a multiple murderer, inevitably emphasizes violence and futility. In *The Strength to Dream*, Wilson attacks Zola for 'writing over-sexed and sordid books and claiming for them some higher scientific or artistic justification'. He claims that all Zola's novels move towards climaxes of violence and sex, while setting out to disarm the reader by adopting a 'precise, objective tone'. By the 'piling up of violence', Zola's novels vanish as works of art and become merely sensational.[3] All these criticisms could apply to *The Killer*.

There are moments in the novel when the oppressive atmosphere lifts and the air of a healthier world enters. The portrait of Pauline, the sister upon whom Lingard has an incestuous fixation, is especially effective. In one respect, she is a female version of Wilson's male heroes in that she encounters sordidness, corruption and violence, but remains essentially untouched:

> This girl was a living equivalent of Joyce's Molly Bloom: intelligent in her way, very alive, naturally sensual . . . she was as naturally above her neighbours as if she had been born a princess. . . . She had become her guardian's mistress at twelve, she had lived in a tiny house with her aunt and cousins . . . and it had left her unscathed. For her, it was all somehow natural.[4]

Lingard's cousin, Aggie, to whom he was very close, is a similar figure. When Kahn meets her at the end of the novel, he calls her 'Blake's "soul of sweet delight" who can never be defiled'.[5] But these incarnations of innocence cannot relieve the overall claustrophobia for very long.

Since *The Killer* does focus so heavily upon Lingard himself, we must ask how successful he is as a portrait of a murderer. We find that the central weakness in the portrait is that of the whole novel: the various aspects that Wilson accumulates, mostly from textbooks and studies of real-life criminals, do not fuse into a convincing unity, although we feel, as we read, that there is the potential for fusion. We noted that Caradoc Cunningham in *Man Without a Shadow*, and George Sundheim in *The Glass Cage*, tended to be collections of attributes rather than realized characters: this is even truer of Lingard. But some aspects of Lingard are well evoked: in particular, the development of his imagination.

As a child, the only reading available to him was magazines such as *Weird Tales* (one of H. P. Lovecraft's principal publishers), *True Detective* and *True Confessions*. He liked a magazine called *Terror Tales* and especially enjoyed science fiction of the 'space opera' kind. His favourite book was a lurid paperback called *Marvo the Magician*. He enjoyed frightening other children in the neighbourhood with stories of ghosts and monsters. The analogy with Wilson's own childhood is clear.

All this reading stimulated Lingard's imagination. He found an outlet for his will-to-power in identifying with Marvo, a man whose magic enabled him to dominate other men. His imaginative faculty developed to such an extent that he had a remarkable vision:

> He was making a map of an area of Martian territory in the kingdom of Jeddak . . . he was aware of a peculiar absorption in his game, a feeling of silence and concentration. Suddenly he began to feel something. . . . An immense sense of contentment rose in him. Then, as he looked at the map of Jeddak, there was a strange sensation of *remembering* it. With a shock he realized that this was not imagination: it was real. He had a sensation of dark hills rising above him, of cliffs that sloped inwards, and had green, glassy markings on their surface, of trees whose foliage was black and glossy, of great red and purple fruits: at the same time, he clearly smelled the air, which was distinctive, and heard the sound of the flowing water. A sense of revelation came over him, of grasping something that was *true*.[6]

This power of vision could make Lingard into an artist or a mystic. Instead, he becomes a murderer.

Lingard's descent into crime is not rendered too convincingly, however. There are certain successes in individual scenes: the descriptions of Lingard's early burglaries, which often involve panty fetishism, effectively convey his mingled feelings of fear, excitement and violation; the account of his first murder, when he batters a homosexual to death, has a certain crude power, though it is questionable whether its power can be distinguished from that of any sensation novel. But the general criticism is, once again, that these accounts do not fuse into a convincing whole.

The difficulties Wilson's attempt to focus closely on a killer creates suggest an important point. The interest in murder displayed in *Ritual in the Dark* and *The Glass Cage* has two main aspects: the study of the murderer, and of the man who is fascinated by the murderer. We are concerned as much, if not more, with the latter as with the former, especially in *Ritual*. In *The Killer*, because of the close focus on Lingard, the study of the man who is fascinated by Lingard has a much smaller place. Thus *The Killer* loses a dimension of interest, and one, moreover, which Wilson's earlier novels may make us feel he is particularly good at exploring.

Furthermore, although we come closer to Lingard in one sense, he is more firmly distanced from us in another. Although Kahn's relationship with Lingard extends well beyond that of psychiatrist to patient, it is inevitably conditioned by Kahn's professional role to some extent. From *Ritual in the Dark* to *The Killer*, we can trace a growing detachment in the portrait of the murderer. Sorme is very close to Nunne; Reade is much more detached from Sundheim; Kahn is the most detached of all, and his role as a prison psychiatrist symbolizes this. To some extent, Lingard is always a 'case'; the 'case' of the man who is fascinated by him is much less fully explored.

It is given some attention, however. The relationship between Kahn and Lingard has some similarities with that between Sorme and Nunne in *Ritual in the Dark*. At first, there is fascination and the attempt to probe an enigma; then the gradual disclosure of a brutal reality; and, finally, rejection. Despite his professional responsibilities, Kahn, like Sorme, is prepared for a long time to protect a murderer from the law:

> Lingard placed me in the strangest dilemma of my whole career. . . . I soon became aware that a dangerous psychopath was being treated as more or less harmless and trustworthy. I knew it was my duty to warn the prison governor. I also knew that if I did so, I would betray the tenuous links of trust that had sprung up between Lingard and myself. I decided that I would take the risk.[7]

At first, Kahn sees Lingard as 'fundamentally a victim of

circumstances', due to his deprived background, and he feels 'sympathy and pity'.[8] As he learns more about him, he realizes Lingard's intelligence, imaginative capacity and will-to-power. He finds himself identifying with Lingard in his reaction, as a child, against a degrading environment. He goes further: he declares that Lingard is 'the most interesting human being I would ever encounter'; he becomes infatuated with him: 'For weeks I talked and thought about nothing but Lingard: I walked around on a cloud, like a lover.'[9]

As Kahn finds out more about Lingard, however, he stresses the role of free choice in his decision to become a criminal; Kahn decides that it was not simply due to environmental pressures, considerable though these were. Like Gustav Neumann, Lingard decides to become a 'great criminal', inspired by reading about Professor Moriarty, Sherlock Holmes's arch-foe. Unlike Neumann, he acts on this decision, with destructive consequences.

Nonetheless, Kahn believes that Lingard can still be saved, can reform and live a purposive life; he continues to believe this even when he learns that Lingard has murdered three men— not for sexual reasons—in addition to the manslaughter for which he is serving his current sentences. But when he realizes that Lingard is a multiple sex killer, he comes to feel about him as Sorme came to feel about Nunne at the end of *Ritual*:

> I had been missing the vital point about him. . . . There could no longer be any question of curing him. Cure him for what? For a lifetime behind bars? *He* understood the problem: that a complete confession would be the equivalent of suicide.[10]

The comments about suicide echo those of Damon Reade on Sundheim in *The Glass Cage*.

The relationship between Kahn and Lingard is, however, nothing like enough to rescue the novel. *The Killer* does not attain its author's stated ends and does not develop the area of interest that had been explored fruitfully, but by no means exhaustively, in *Ritual* and *The Glass Cage*: the fascination with murder. Moreover, *The Killer* is too much like a 'shilling shocker'; this objection stands, despite Wilson's attempt to defuse it in his 'Introduction'. *Ritual*, *The Glass Cage* and *The World of Violence* certainly contain sensational elements, but they are clearly more than sensation novels. But in the documentary detail which constitutes it as an attempt at a 'nonfiction novel', and in the quality of its prose, *The Killer* is uncomfortably close to sensation fiction—even down to clichés such as 'made him feel like a hungry wild animal', 'His heart leapt with joy' (on seeing a pair of white panties), 'he loathed him with every atom of his being', 'bloody pulp', 'full horror'.[11]

In *The Killer*, various sensation magazines and novels are invoked: *True Detective*, *True Confessions*, a boxing novel called *The Kid from Louisville*. This novel has a shattering effect on Lingard because it describes sex with a beautiful woman who has the same name as Lingard's sister. Wilson provides an extract from it:

> He leaned forward, took her lip between his teeth, and bit it so the blood came. One jerk of his big hand tore away the flimsy panties and tossed them into the fire. His other hand reached up under the dress, and tore loose the black bra.[12]

The invocation of sensational texts highlights the question of the relationship between them and *The Killer*. The conclusion must be: despite Wilson's different intentions, *The Killer* comes too close to such texts, and at times is indistinguishable from them. It exemplifies the danger in Wilson's use of popular materials in his novels: they may overwhelm his serious concerns.

After the claustrophobically narrow focus of *The Killer*, *The God of the Labyrinth* (1970) broadens the field of vision considerably. It is a combination of a tale of literary research—a 'literary detective story', as Wilson calls it[13]—a pornographic novel and a story of the supernatural: these merge into a parable of evolutionary existentialism. The story is told in the first person by the hero of *Ritual in the Dark* and *Man Without A Shadow*, Gerard Sorme: the *persona* for Wilson himself. The use of the diary form in the opening pages of the novel emphasizes its continuity from *Man Without A Shadow*, before we move into a non-diary first-person narrative. In the earlier novel, we saw Sorme developing an awareness of an order underlying the empirical, contingent surface of the world. At the very beginning of *The God of the Labyrinth*, Sorme affirms his belief in such an order, saying 'Now I eagerly follow the lead of coincidence', and

123

as the novel progresses, he will move deeper and deeper into the occult realities beneath the everyday world.[14]

Sorme is still married to Diana, the woman whom he won from Kirsten in *Man Without A Shadow*; they now have a three-year-old daughter. But this does not cramp Sorme's sexual style. While on a lecture tour of America, he is approached by an American publisher who intends to publish the 'sex diary' of Esmond Donelly, an eighteenth-century Irish rake. The publisher offers him a large sum to write an Introduction and research into Donelly's background. At first, Sorme is reluctant; he reads the diary, and decides that Donelly is 'just a dirty-minded ruffian'.[15] But the publisher uses an attractive young girl to persuade him to accept.

Sorme soon discovers that the diary he has read is a forgery; Donelly's real diary reveals that he was a man of high intelligence whose preoccupations, despite the gap of two centuries, are very close to Sorme's. Sorme also learns of Donelly's connection with a mysterious 'Sect of the Phoenix'—Wilson has pointed out that he developed the idea of this sect from a hint by Jorge Luis Borges.[16] Like Sorme, Donelly saw sex not as an end in itself but as a means of attaining the experience of power, meaning and purpose, and defeating the 'dark god' who keeps men trapped in the 'labyrinth' of the everyday.[17] The novel becomes the story of the quest for Donelly, as *Necessary Doubt* was the story of the quest for Neumann, and Donelly, though a man of the eighteenth century, is, like Neumann, a herald of the twenty-first.

Like Neumann, Donelly is at first an elusive figure, seen through a glass darkly. Distant by two centuries, he is even more elusive. But gradually, the clouded glass clears, as Sorme acquires eighteenth-century documents by or about Donelly. He gets hold of these in various ways, which usually involve some sexual adventure. Sorme's exploits in this area add a new dimension to literary research; he is a scholar-adventurer with a difference.

Extracts from these documents are inserted into Sorme's narrative. Wilson's novels have incorporated frame tales before, but these have been narrated in a style like that of the main text. But with Donelly, though his ideas may be like his creator's, the language of the documents produced by or about him in his physical lifetime must necessarily be different from Wilson's usual prose. In particular, they cannot employ those images drawn from later nineteenth- and twentieth-century technology to which Wilson is so prone. This produces a refreshing variation in the style of *The God of the Labyrinth*.

As Sorme's quest continues, he begins to find unexpected help: from Donelly himself. This is an extension of an experience that any scholar engaged in literary research may have: the sense of becoming, momentarily, the writer he is studying; seeing with his eyes, thinking in his words. But in Sorme's case, it is more than intense imaginative empathy: his mind and Donelly's are really interpenetrating:

> I knew I was driving through a small hamlet called Fardrum, a few miles beyond Athlone, and that I intended to stop at the pub at Moate for a ham sandwich and a draught Guinness. At the same time, I was seated beside the coachman on the box of a jolting coach, smelling the lathery sweat of the horses and the clean air of an April morning, as well as the tang of peat smoke from the clothes of the driver.[18]

Wilson presents this as a real possibility, a 'thought experiment'.

For Sorme, the 'double-consciousness' effect demonstrates two truths: that 'time is an illusion',[19] in that the mind, if not the body, can travel back through time, as Howard Lester's did in *The Philosopher's Stone*; and that life after death is a reality—the position that Wilson himself now maintains. For Sorme is not only looking into Donelly's past mind: that mind still exists in the present. Thus *The God of the Labyrinth* becomes a story of the supernatural, or rather, of an expanded concept of the natural. Wilson makes Sorme recognize the move into the supernatural genre when he has him say:

> it struck me that Sheridan Le Fanu might have written a powerful and gloomy story about the double-tenancy of a human brain by two men of different centuries.[20]

For Sorme, however, the experience is not gloomy, but liberating, especially at this point:

> Esmond and I ceased to be two men inhabiting the same body, and were suddenly identified. . . . It brought a feeling of

125

tremendous delight and freedom. It was like being let out of a coalmine. What had suddenly vanished was that basic fear that enters the mind of all intelligent people at some time in their lives: that they are really the only person in the universe, that life is an elaborate joke, a film show created by a bored god who knows he is alone, and who has given himself amnesia to forget his loneliness. For here was Esmond's consciousness, as undeniably real and elaborate as my own, mingled with my own.[21]

This experience frees Sorme from the solipsist trap. It does more: it reveals some of the potentialities of the men of the future. This tale that appears to look backwards is really looking forwards: a supernatural device becomes the symbol of some aspects of the 'evolutionary leap', as a science fiction device was in *Necessary Doubt* and *The Philosopher's Stone*: it promotes the novel to the level of evolutionary parable. Esmond, speaking through Sorme, says:

> Sorme will succeed [in moving into the next evolutionary phase]. And when a dozen men have succeeded, the rest of the human race will follow.[22]

If this parable stays closer to earth and seems less arbitrary than *The Mind Parasites* and *The Philosopher's Stone*, this is partly due to the structuring provided by its 'literary detective story', and, perhaps more significantly, to its use of the conventions of the pornographic novel.

In his 'Note' which follows *The God of the Labyrinth*, Wilson contends that the pornographic novel is 'more rigidly formalized than any other type'.[23] In addition to its structural function, the pornographic element in *The God of the Labyrinth* has two further functions. As Sorme recognized in *Man Without A Shadow*, sex has a double nature, both uplifting and debasing; to write in a way that invoked the conventions of pornography but rose above them would be to symbolize this. Moreover, it would awaken the energy of sexuality, but direct it into a higher channel: both stir and sublimate. This would need very careful handling of the pornographic conventions, however; Wilson attempts this particularly risky operation in *The God of the Labyrinth*. As in *The Killer*, though far less frequently, there are times when Wilson fuses with his model, and the effect is distasteful, the humour crude. On the whole, however, he holds his balance on the tightrope.

It is in *The God of the Labyrinth* that Wilson comes closest to his stated aim of achieving 'an effect approximating to parody' in his use of popular forms. Most of the sexual exploits are redeemed by the humour of parody, and by a bawdy relish. For example, this, from Sorme's account of his visit to a descendant of Esmond's, Colonel Donelly, in quest of documents:

> Donelly talked on and on, detailing his experiences in the brothels of the world. The man had so many fixations and perversions that it would take another twenty pages to detail them—women's hair, patent leather shoes (women's) . . . razor blades. . . . Towards midnight, he showed me his collection of guns, of obscene photographs, and of whips and canes. He handed me a cat-o'-nine-tails and asked me to try it. I swished it through the air, and he closed his eyes as if he was listening to delightful music. Then he said dreamily: 'Would you like to use it?'
>
> 'On you?' I had guessed this was what he was leading up to. 'Yes.'
>
> 'No. I'd feel silly.'
>
> He gripped my arm.
>
> 'Not even in exchange for the manuscript?'
>
> 'You'd let me take it?'
>
> 'You could copy it and return it.'
>
> 'All right.'
>
> His voice became a croak.
>
> 'Come in here.'[24]

The parodic effect is enhanced by Sorme's essential detachment from his sexual adventures, his constant tendency to intellectualize them, as well as everything else. When Esmond Donelly, again speaking through Sorme, says: 'Like myself, Mr. Sorme is not basically interested in sex. He is something of a Puritan', it may seem highly comic, in view of Sorme's exploits; but in a sense, it is true.[25]

The parody, bawdy, and Sorme's essential detachment contribute to an alienation effect, though there is a peculiar tension between this, and the erotically involving effect of the pornography, at least for heterosexual male readers.

Sorme's quest for Donelly and the Sect of the Phoenix

becomes, through the interpenetration of their minds, a quest with Donelly: the relationship between men with a common mission, seen in some of Wilson's previous novels, is now internalized. After several adventures, Sorme comes to a country house where group sessions for sexual therapy are being held. There, helped by Donelly, Sorme achieves that prolongation of sexual energy aimed at by Caradoc Cunningham in *Man Without A Shadow*: he makes love to many women, one after another. In his account of this remarkable feat, Wilson fuses humour, reverence, direct presentation and analytic commentary: both the humour and the commentary count towards an alienation effect.

Sorme's feat is a successful version of the 'sexual magic' that Cunningham tried to demonstrate in *Man Without A Shadow*, but at a more serious level, and without mumbo-jumbo (both of these features help to account for its success). Sorme earnestly endeavours to make its seriousness clear to us; as he says, 'Esmond was not doing this for fun. On one level, this was a demonstration.'[26] It is a demonstration of man's hidden powers, which could promote him on to the next evolutionary plane. Sex is a way, but only one way, of releasing those powers. The demonstration finally becomes vision:

> As I looked around this room of naked goddesses, a deep joy rose in me. These were the mothers, the procreators of the race, whom men have always enslaved and degraded. I worshipped them as divinities. Their loins are man's entrance to the world of dreams, of greatness, of the primeval purpose that lies behind matter. I saw no distinction between them, between the young and pretty and the tense middle-aged. The desire to serve them all was impersonal and free of lust. I stood up, and took the hand of a thin, neurotic-looking girl who had been waiting; we moved over to the corner of the room. A part of my being stood behind an altar draped in red velvet, in a temple of carved sandstone; I wore a mask in the shape of the head of a great bird. Forty naked women stood in a row before the congregation; their bodies shone with oil, and each held in her hand a phial in which glowed a green, effervescent·liquid whose nature I suddenly understood.[27]

After this peak of sexual-mystical experience, Sorme meets the present Grand Master of the Sect of the Phoenix, a

Turkish millionaire called Xalide Nuri. Donelly speaks through Sorme to tell Nuri that he has outgrown sex, for the pursuit of which the Sect of the Phoenix was originally founded; like Don Juan in Shaw's *Man and Superman*, he has moved on to higher things. He emphasizes that once someone has achieved sufficient control over the will and the consciousness, it is 'almost impossible to die'.[28] Above all, he emphasizes the evolutionary imperative.

Sorme concludes the novel with an anecdote in which Nuri's blind sage, Boris, is asked where Esmond Donelly is now: 'Boris's sightless face turned to me: "He is Esmond".'[29]

There is a hint of reincarnation here; but the essential points are those Sorme made earlier in the novel: that time is an illusion, and death unnecessary. *The Mind Parasites* moved too far away from the human and physical world and from any clearly structured alternative worlds to make these points effectively. In *The God of the Labyrinth*, which is anchored by the novelistic conventions within which it works, they come across much more strongly.

The God of the Labyrinth is one of Wilson's most effective novels. Perhaps it should be seen as the non-realistic complement to *Ritual in the Dark*: the use of Sorme as the hero reinforces the comparison and contrast. *Man Without A Shadow* might be regarded as the transitional work linking *Ritual* and *God*; in *Shadow*, Sorme moves from an existential to an evolutionary view of reality. Both *Ritual* and *God* are on a larger scale than Wilson's other novels, with the possible exception of *The Black Room*: both make special demands on Wilson's prose—*Ritual* because of its detailed realism and its stream-of-consciousness passages, *The God of the Labyrinth* because of the supposedly eighteenth-century documents that it incorporates. Both have qualities of spaciousness and light, despite the potentially debasing nature of some of the material they handle. Both contain much humour. Both weave their expository, didactic aspects into a larger whole. In *Ritual*, however, the affirmation of a non-empirical reality is tentative and provisional; in *The God of the Labyrinth*, such a reality is affirmed from the start and is explored as the novel progresses into modes of being beyond the conventions of the everyday world. *Ritual* explores existence; *The God of the Labyrinth*, evolution.

In *The Black Room* (1971), Wilson turns from the porno-graphic novel to the spy novel. Once more, it is a risky choice. Wilson has said himself that some of the James Bond stories—which are the epitome of modern spy fiction—seem to him like 'real pornography' because, like the gangster novels he read as a child, they present a 'world without values'.[30] As with *The Killer* and *The God of the Labyrinth*, Wilson chooses a mode that is generally perceived as debasing and tries to elevate it, to make it, in some way, a vehicle for values.

As Karl Zweig and Damon Reade were unlikely detectives, so the hero of *The Black Room*, Kit Butler, is an unlikely spy. We have met a character called Kit Butler before: Damon Reade's friend in *The Glass Cage*: but the hero of the later novel, though he resembles his namesake in that he is a composer and an effortless seducer of women, is, in other respects, dissimilar. We do not feel, for example, that 'the emotional side of his per-sonality' displays 'a painful nostalgia, a haunted death-laden romanticism'.[31] This Kit Butler is, in fact, the typical Wilson hero, with Wilson's own concerns. We are even told that he once wrote: 'Men are like grandfather clocks driven by watch-springs'—a phrase attributed to Gerard Sorme in *Man Without A Shadow* and 'Lord Leicester' in *The Mind Parasites*.[32]

Butler is inveigled into joining a specially-selected group who are being tested to see how long they can resist the acute sensory deprivation experienced in the soundproof, lightproof 'black room'. The group is organized by the intelligence networks of England and America. Butler soon finds that he can resist the room far better than anyone else in the group. He is persuaded to let himself be used as bait for a mysterious 'Station K', an organization that trades in secrets between governments, but is itself independent of any government. It kidnaps secret agents, brainwashes them by means of the black room, then sends them back to infiltrate their own espionage networks. Naturally, all the major nations want it destroyed. Butler's quest for Station K takes him from Scotland to Paris to Prague to the Czecho-slovakian mountains, where he finally enters the headquarters of the strange organization and meets their leader. The varied settings are effectively evoked, and the book conveys a stronger sense of the physical world than any of Wilson's novels since *Ritual*, even though the detail is sometimes banal.

The idea of the black room serves as a focus both for the popular form action of the novel and for Wilson's own pre-occupations. As with *The Mind Parasites*, the seed for the novel seems to have been planted in *Introduction to the New Existentialism*: one chapter of that book is called 'Inside the Dark Room', and deals with the real-life black room experiments at Princeton University in America.[33] In that chapter, Wilson points out that the black room can cause extreme demoralization and panic, making people susceptible to brainwashing, but can also release inner powers which can, for example, cure colds, but which could, Wilson believes, do a good deal more. The black room demonstrates the powers of 'intentionality', and it is a matter of using these in the right way. We said in Chapter Two that the black room is an important symbol for Wilson: it is a crisis situation, one of what the philosopher Jaspers called 'boundary situations' on the edge of everyday life, in which man can either fall deeper or raise himself higher, can achieve, in fact, that independence of the physical world, through the release of hidden mental powers, which is, for Wilson, the distinctive feature of the next stage of human evolution. The idea of the black room also corresponds to some of Wilson's deepest personal obsessions. In his autobiography, he has said that 'the symbol of my childhood was . . . the tub of Diogenes' and spoken of his desire to 'establish complete independence'.[34] The black room is the technological equivalent of the tub of Diogenes, of the cell of the medieval anchorite, and of the darkened attic inhabited by Uncle Sam in *The World of Violence*.

When he is first asked to take part in the black room experiments, Butler believes that resistance to the room is impossible because values would collapse when human beings are thrown back completely on their own subjectivity. Once he is in the room, however, he finds that he is able to summon values from a deeper level of the mind, without any external stimuli. He argues that the answer to the black room problem is to learn to summon 'energy of emergency'—the sense of power, meaning and purpose that is provoked by a sudden crisis—even in the absence of emergency. Butler finds that the techniques he learns in the black room carry over into his everyday life; he is much less subject to the fluctuations of everyday consciousness.

131

Butler believes in the evolutionary importance of his discovery; but the spy agencies of England, America and Russia, who are temporarily combining to try and destroy Station K, want to make use of that discovery for their own short-term purposes. They represent the 'world without values' of the modern spy story; Butler stands for evolutionary values, in Wilson's terms the highest kind. After a spy is killed, Butler stresses this:

> Do you realize that this project concerns human evolution, and that it's one of the most important questions the human race has ever dealt with? And here these damned fools are thinking in terms of espionage and counter espionage and murder. . . . I've simply nothing in common with these people and their vicious values. They take death for granted as part of the game. And it's the one thing I refuse to take for granted.[35]

Butler shares with most of Wilson's previous heroes an inner detachment from the events in which he gets involved; but in his case, as with Sorme in *The God of the Labyrinth*, his detachment is strengthened and validated by his sense of evolutionary purpose, and by the contrast between that purpose and the world of espionage and power politics. Ernst Staufmann, the head of Station K, puts it to Butler that the world's espionage networks are now more important than governments; in *The Black Room* as a whole, they are representative of the worst tendencies of governments—representative of the political world that Wilson rejects. When 'Colonel Sampson', a high-ranking security officer, says: 'Spying's become completely amoral since the end of the second world war—the cold war period', his comments, within the context of the novel, seem to reflect upon governments as well.[36] In his unexpected role as a spy, Butler encounters various forms of commitment—that of the British agent, Ramsay, to King and Country, of the Czech literary critic Hostovsky to East European hard-line Communism, of the young Czech music student Ruzena to a form of Maoism—but he remains detached from them all.

> I agree with your revolutionary idealism. But it's pointed in the wrong direction. You can't save yourself from the horrors of ordinary living with a lot of vague ideas. You've got to understand exactly what prevents you from being free.[37]

At a dinner in Prague, he makes his position clear, at the same time meeting a charge that has sometimes been laid against Wilson himself:

> 'Freedom is mental intensity. Most men are incapable of mental intensity. So most men can never be free.' Ruzena said indignantly: 'That is fascism.' Butler said: 'I don't care what it is. It's true.'[38]

In *The Black Room*, Wilson creates a microcosm of the political world as he sees it and persuades us of the validity of Butler's attitude—and of his own.

In the course of the novel, Butler encounters three larger-than-life figures, of three successive orders of magnitude. Varborg is a spy working for the C.I.A.; a big, powerful, scarred man. Gradwohl is a professor of psychology, who has succeeded in staying in the black room for eleven days. In two vivid frame tales, he gives Butler an account of two of his mountaineering experiences on the north face of the Eiger—the Eigerwand—and tells him of the two lessons he learnt from those experiences: that 'man is as strong as his sense of purpose' and that 'life is only worth living when the will is concentrated.'[39] He appeals to Butler as a partner in a common cause:

> For two million years man has been climbing a mountain of evolution, and his will is so weak that he dies when he is less than a century old. That is all very well for most people, because they are so stupid. But you and I ought to know better, because our business is evolution.[40]

Butler recognizes that Gradwohl represents a kind of evolutionary strength although, as the above statement shows, there is something ambivalent about such strength in purely human terms. Watching him one night at dinner, Butler

> observed that Gradwohl drank only water, and ignored the conversation; it was clear that people and wine were stimulants that he found equally unnecessary. Watching his face, Butler thought of the Eigerwand, and felt a cold surge of delight.[41]

Gradwohl advises Butler not to get mixed up in spying. Butler, however, has become intrigued by certain things he has heard about Station K and he wonders if it is a purely commercial organization, or whether it may not have more idealistic aims. This is why he lets himself be used as bait.

The third larger-than-life figure Butler meets is the head of Station K, Staufmann. When Varborg is captured and brought to Station K, Butler is able to compare the two men:

> Before he had met Staufmann, Varborg was one of the biggest men he had seen. Both were over six feet tall; both were powerfully built; both were scarred. But there was a fundamental difference between them that was inexpressible in words, a difference in the quality of their vitality. Varborg's strength was that of an explorer or a mountain climber, although its outlines had been blurred by lack of challenge. Staufmann's peculiar quality was scarcely human; as he looked down at Varborg's face, he reminded Butler of some great saurian of a past age, peering out of its cave at an intruder, curious but totally certain of its own power. The slack skin of the neck, the twisted face, all seemed nonhuman.[42]

Staufmann is the largest scale figure in the novel, a fact symbolized by his physical pre-eminence; Gradwohl ranks in between Varborg and Staufmann. Like Gustav Neumann at the end of *Necessary Doubt*, though to an even greater extent, Staufmann is a powerful, compelling, enigmatic figure, a disturbing image of the future. Much more than Gradwohl, he focuses the ambivalence of the superman idea, its nonhuman aspect.

Staufmann clearly respects Butler, especially in view of Butler's capacity to withstand the black room, and sets out to impress him. Though Butler does not wholly trust Staufmann, he recognizes his power. Staufmann tells Butler that he has 'a crazy obsession with the problem of human greatness'.[43] There are hints, however, that his will-to-greatness is distorted insofar as it shows itself as an interest in political power. Staufmann was a close friend of Hitler's before the war and, according to Varborf, ran Hitler's Special Intelligence Service during it. Staufmann minimizes this latter role, but, in the most extensive and fascinating frame tale in the novel, he gives Butler and Ruzena an account of his friendship with Hitler.

The portrait of Hitler he presents is ambivalent. It is not the monster-buffoon of popular myth, but a man of will, energy and idealism which has been forced into the wrong channels.

Staufmann says, for example, that Hitler 'deliberately culti-
vated will-power until it acquired the force of a dynamo'.[44] In
view of the positive associations of such words as 'will-power'
and 'dynamo' in Wilson's work, Staufmann's Hitler is clearly
not an altogether evil or contemptible figure. While Staufmann's account is not presented to us as wholly reliable, it
nonetheless suggests that Hitler was, to some extent, an
example of a frustrated dynamic energy and will that could
have been used to benefit rather than harm mankind: the same
point that Wilson makes about a certain kind of murderer.

Staufmann also tells Butler about Station K, which he
describes as a kind of 'religious community'.[45] Certainly life
there is highly disciplined: austere diet, vigorous physical
exercise, concentration sessions, a rigorous programme of
language learning, all form part of its routines. One of the
functions of this discipline, however, is to make Station K's
men, and women, into better secret agents. Staufmann endeavours to convince Butler that Station K's aims are idealistic, that it represents 'my own small attempt to change the
course of history'.[46] Ruzena is converted, but Butler remains
uncertain. Like Zweig with Neumann at the end of *Necessary
Doubt*, Butler cannot wholly credit Staufmann's plea in his
own defence. His main doubts revolve around the political
aspect of Staufmann's aims, which link his idealism too closely
with the amoral world of power politics. Staufmann's association with Hitler has obvious relevance to such doubts.

As the novel draws to a close, Butler joins some of Station
K's agents when they go to kidnap Gomolyka, the head of the
K.G.B. whom Butler has previously met in Paris. Gomolyka is
returning to Moscow to arrange for Russian troops to move
into Czechoslovakia and seize Station K. The kidnap of
Gomolyka will mean that Staufmann has now captured all
those who set out to capture him; he already has Butler,
Varborg and Ramsay. Waiting with the Station K agents for
Gomolyka's car to approach, holding a gun, Butler has an
experience of detachment, of otherness, of a new control over
time: the Faculty X experience:

> Absurdly, the weight of cold metal in his hand brought a
> sudden hallucinatory memory of a perfume; it was so distinct

that it might have been sprinkled on the furry lining of the collar that was now damp with his breath. It was the perfume that Jane had been wearing when she had said goodbye on Victoria Station; he had intended to ask her its name. This clear sense of another time and place brought with it a feeling of affirmation and detachment. He was intensely aware of the night, of the trees, of the flowing water and the snow-covered stones at the edge of the stream, and also of his own identity suspended among these things. But it seemed unimportant whether he was there or elsewhere. It was as if he could make time stand still by an act of concentration.[47]

The next moment, the car carrying Gomolyka rounds the bend and is stopped by one of Station K's agents, disguised as a Czech policeman. The sentence 'The car stopped', indented like the start of a new paragraph, stops the novel, abruptly: the popular form action remains unresolved, and our expectations on this level are disappointed, compelling us to consider the novel in its other, higher identity, as a parable of evolutionary existentialism. On that level, the ending marks a new beginning, a new stage in Butler's development. In Chapter Seven, we cited Wilson's suggestion for a type of novel that would 'move on the level of a story, but end by bringing the reader to reality'.[48] At the end of *The Black Room*, Butler has, in Wilson's terms, risen to the level of reality; he both stays within the story and transcends it, and the story hangs unresolved, perpetually in motion but always immobilized, forever constraining the hero but constantly releasing him. Butler has achieved a kind of transcendent reality, and the reality at the political level—or at the level of a spy novel, the implication being that the two have much in common—is seen in its proper perspective. For all that, Butler remains in the world; decisions, choices, still have to be made; but these are left open-ended.

The Black Room is a successful use of the spy novel for serious ends. It succeeds better than *The God of the Labyrinth* in that it never falls to the level of the popular form it employs. Espionage provides Wilson with a symbol of the 'world without values' and of the political world; in contrast, the positive nature of the hero's evolutionary quest shows up more strongly, and his rejection of political commitment seems more admirable than evasive. The close attention to the detail of the physical world helps to give credibility to the spy plot, and makes Butler's states of heightened consciousness more convincing because they, so to speak, take off from the world that we know. The conventions of the spy plot also help to provide a framework that prevents Butler from soaring too far into the empyrean. We do not get that exclusion of the shared human world epitomized in *The Mind Parasites* and *The Philosopher's Stone*. The concept of the black room is an effective focus for the spy action and for Wilson's evolutionary concerns. As in *Necessary Doubt*, the ambivalence of the superman idea is brought out, especially in the portrayal of Staufmann, and the open ending of the novel is a recognition that the implications of evolutionary ideas on the political and social level are complex and not easily resolved. This contrasts with the disregard of such difficulties in Wilson's previous science fiction works. At the end of *The Black Room*, as in *Necessary Doubt* but to a greater extent, we are left with a more complex sense of the world: this gives greater depth to the expression of Wilson's evolutionary optimism in the novel. *The Black Room* is a promising start to his second decade as a published novelist.

NOTES

1. 'Introduction', *The Killer* (New English Library, 1970; my refs. to Panther, 1977 ed.), pp. 5–6.
2. 'Introduction', *Killer*, p. 10.
3. *Strength to Dream*, pp. 49–50.
4. *Killer*, p. 58.
5. *Killer*, p. 219.
6. *Killer*, p. 99.
7. *Killer*, p. 13.
8. *Killer*, p. 64.
9. *Killer*, p. 140.
10. *Killer*, p. 200.
11. *Killer*, pp. 105, 167, 181, 203.
12. *Killer*, p. 38.
13. 'Note', *God of the Labyrinth*, p. 284.
14. *God of the Labyrinth*, p. 10.
15. *God*, p. 20.
16. 'Note', *God*, p. 284.
17. *God*, pp. 131, 132.

18. *God*, p. 135.
19. *God*, p. 135.
20. *God*, p. 138.
21. *God*, p. 237.
22. *God*, p. 270.
23. 'Note', *God*, p. 284.
24. *God*, pp. 44–5.
25. *God*, p. 271.
26. *God*, p. 243.
27. *God*, p. 244.
28. *God*, p. 271.
29. *God*, p. 274.
30. 'Note', *God*, p. 278.
31. *Glass Cage*, p. 60.
32. *The Black Room* (Weidenfeld & Nicolson, 1971; my refs. to Sphere, 1971; my refs. to Sphere, 1977 ed.), p. 61. Cf. *Mind Parasites*, p. 81.
33. *Intro to New Existm*, pp. 115–18, 130.
34. *Voyage*, p. 23.
35. *Black Room*, p. 122.
36. *Black Room*, p. 92.
37. *Black Room*, p. 162.
38. *Black Room*, p. 178.
39. *Black Room*, pp. 66, 67.
40. *Black Room*, p. 67.
41. *Black Room*, p. 105.
42. *Black Room*, pp. 278–79.
43. *Black Room*, p. 237.
44. *Black Room*, p. 237.
45. *Black Room*, p. 221.
46. *Black Room*, p. 236.
47. *Black Room*, p. 298.
48. See Chapter Seven, n. 8.

9

The Story So Far

In the eleven years from 1960 to 1971, Colin Wilson produced eleven novels. In the ten years from 1972 to 1982, he has published only two. These are slight works, and do not require a great deal of comment. They do not give a sense of development, but of a reworking, on a narrower basis, of old themes.

The Schoolgirl Murder Case (1974) was, Wilson says, consciously written as a kind of Maigret novel.[1] The hero, Chief Superintendent Saltfleet, is a lightly characterized 'philosophical' policeman, akin to Simenon's famous detective, or Alan Hunter's Gently. The plot involves the characteristic Wilsonian motifs of sexual crime and deviance (the 'schoolgirl' murder victim is in fact a prostitute in her twenties dressed in school uniform), and black and white magic. The relationship between Saltfleet and Madame Galleti, a medium, and his reliance on the information she gains by apparently occult means, are interesting; but in general, the novel has a kind of anonymity: it might be by anyone. The only stimulating question above the crime-and-detection level is raised at the end, when Saltfleet says of the murderer: 'I know [he's] a murderous little bastard. But that's not what I mean. . . . *Why* is he a murderous little bastard?'[2] To explore that question further, however, we must turn to Wilson's earlier novels. *The Schoolgirl Murder Case* might have a certain value in sending readers who are unfamiliar with Wilson's other fiction to those novels; otherwise, it is successful only on the level on which it was favourably reviewed: as a police detective thriller.

The Space Vampires (1976) is another excursion into science fiction—or more precisely, into science fantasy. It is less ambitious than *The Mind Parasites* or *The Philosopher's Stone*: it does not offer an extensive projection of evolved man. There are successful moments: the opening of the novel, when a group of spacemen from earth discover an immense ship containing humanoid life-forms in a state of suspended animation; the evocation of the hero's first encounter with an awakened vampire in the form of an attractive female; the account which the alien life-forces, speaking through human bodies, give of themselves. As in the previous science fiction novels, there is much description of telepathic intuition, the exercise of 'will-pressure', the possession of one mind by another; these suffer from the same drawbacks as those novels; they are not especially evocative and they have an arbitrary air; we are, once again, in that region where anything can happen. Furthermore, like *The Schoolgirl Murder Case*, this novel has an anonymous quality: some of it might be a transcription of an episode of *Star Trek*.

Even more than *The Killer*, both these novels demonstrate the danger of the popular form method. Despite its sordidness, *The Killer* had a certain power, a distinctive stamp; these two novels are, simply, popular fiction. In one respect, they are more technically successful than some of H. G. Wells's later fiction, because they do succeed to some degree on the popular form level; but they also seem more trivial. To use a phrase of Saint-Beuve's that Wilson is fond of quoting, they are 'books that one reads with one hand'.[3]

Wilson will certainly have more novels to offer us. Last year (1981), he completed a novel called *The Magician from Siberia*. The novel takes the form of a dramatized popular biography, and its subject is a figure who clearly fascinates Wilson: Grigory Rasputin, the monk who, in pre-revolutionary Russia, rose from peasant stock to become the confidant of the Tsarina and a power behind the throne. Wilson has already written a straightforward biography of Rasputin (*Rasputin and the Fall of the Romanovs*, 1964), and he also discusses him in *The Occult*.

The most successful part of the novel is its account of Rasputin's boyhood and youth. From an early age, he becomes conscious of an ability to sink into mystical states, and of the fact that he possesses 'strange powers', such as healing and precognition. The evocations of his wanderings in steppe and forest, of the mystical 'kinship with the earth' that he enjoys, call to mind the novels of Hermann Hesse and Knut Hamsun. They remind us of the strong Romantic impulse in Wilson's nature. The later part of the novel, dealing with Rasputin's life after he has become the confidant of the Tsarina, is less successful: much more attention is given to narrating external events than to evoking Rasputin's inner states, which had been Wilson's main concern in the first part of the novel. It may be that this reflects the fact that, for Wilson, Rasputin's later life is less interesting, since he failed to develop his inner powers. Although Rasputin's involvement in the political life of pre-revolutionary Russia is complex and fascinating, Wilson has always acknowledged his relative lack of interest in politics so that, although he narrates Rasputin's political involvement with clarity and competence, we do not feel that his energies are fully engaged.

Wilson also has a 'work in progress' on which he has worked intermittently since the early 1960s. It was originally conceived as a novel on the force of sex, a force symbolized by Lulu—a figure whom Wilson had encountered in Frank Wedekind's two *Lulu* plays, and in Alban Berg's opera of the same title. In the present version of the novel, the hero is a young man called Theodore Pelham; Theodore has many fascinating characteristics. He is a kind of Prince Myshkin figure; a naturally superb athlete; the possessor of a photographic memory; the heir to a peerage and a huge racing stable. Most important of all, he has the capacity to inwardly rise above normal human problems; he has almost instant access to the source of mystical experience. In this, he embodies what Wilson now sees as the central theme of the novel: the power of the human mind to transcend the everyday world.

We will not go into the details of the plot here, which are, in any case, still in the process of being worked out. The action of the novel is intended to take place over a year, from October 1967 until the autumn of 1968, and it includes, among other things, Theo's arrival at medical school, to which he has gained entrance by memorizing the whole of *Gray's Anatomy*; his encounter with Lulu in the form of the beautiful 16-year-old stepdaughter of a suicide; his initial loss of Lulu when his mother's lover runs away with her; his re-acquaintance with his titled father, whom he has not seen since childhood; and his involvement with an extreme leftist group, rather like the Angry Brigade. It can be seen that these elements could make for a most interesting story.

Wilson has run into two main difficulties with the novel, however. First, all Wilson's published novels which are told in the third, as distinct from the first, person, take place over a short period of time. The only exception to this is *The Glass Cage*, but that is divided into two short time-spans, with a clean break in between. *Lulu*, however, is intended to cover a comparatively long period of time, and this has presented Wilson with problems of selection and compression that he has not faced in his previously published third person works.

The second problem is more important, since it relates to the central theme of the novel, which is exemplified by Theo's ability to inwardly transcend normal human problems. The difficulty this presents is twofold: how to convey this inner state of transcendence, and how to combine it with the narrative demand, the will-to-action, of the plot of the novel. It is a problem which, as we have seen, Wilson has faced, to some extent, in other novels: most particularly in *The Glass Cage*, where, as we saw in Chapter Six, Reade's ability to attain mystical states very quickly, and to detach himself from the events in which he is involved, gives that novel a curiously static quality.

If Wilson can tackle these problems successfully, however, it could be that this work in progress, with its richness of action and its metaphysical explorations, will become his most substantial novel since *Ritual in the Dark*. Like *Ritual*, it will be the product of many years' thought and work, and may thus be more deeply imbued with his major preoccupations than his other post-*Ritual* novels. Unlike *Ritual*, it will be the product not of youth, but of maturity. Wilson has said that he really needs two or three years to complete this novel: we must hope that he finds the time.

Let us now, however, make a provisional attempt to sum up Wilson's achievement on the basis of his published novels. Wilson has always been driven by a powerful set of obsessions. He claims that these obsessions are central to the human condition, and there is no doubt that they correspond, in many respects, to the concerns of traditional religious and mystical thought. But in his novels, they can produce a certain narrowness. Kenneth Allsop commented on Wilson in 1958: 'His thinking is formidable in its own chosen routes . . . yet there are vast areas it has never encountered.'[5] This remains true: and it refers to areas of experience as well as of thought. We saw in Chapter Three Wilson's argument that the novelist should aim to develop wide-angle consciousness, a 'bird's-eye view' of life; but there are whole areas of life that his novels ignore. All present-day novelists have a limited range in comparison with their great nineteenth-century predecessors, because they can no longer believe they have a central cultural role; and Wilson's limitations are more evident because they lie in those areas of which the twentieth century has become particularly, perhaps excessively conscious: personal relationships, society, and politics. Nonetheless, the effect of narrowness is strong in Wilson's novels, and it is inevitably increased by his didacticism and his insistence on optimism.

This insistence on optimism entails a willed self-insulation from those aspects of life which can be subsumed under the heading: human suffering. Like it or not, human suffering forms, at this point in time, and in all the past times of which we have authoritative record, a major part of the human condition. Wilson criticizes writers who suggest that suffering is the whole truth of the human condition; but he goes too far in the other direction. He seems insufficiently 'disturbed by life'.[6]

This lack of openness to the negative side of human existence is combined with a lack, or a suppression, of 'negative capability' in Keats's sense—the capacity to be in 'uncertainties, mysteries, doubts'.[7] He flies too quickly to solutions; his certainties seem to be gained with too little effort. Nigel Dennis has commented: 'Mr. Wilson suffers from having no doubts, and the defect is damaging to his intelligence.'[8] Now it seems clear enough that Wilson has, at certain times in his life, been prone to acute doubts—the 'vastations'—and that fighting them has developed in him a habit of consistently repressing doubts. This habit gives him a kind of strength; but to some extent, it damages him as a novelist. As a young man, Wilson stated:

I see my problem as this: to start from Eliot's '[pessimistic] sense

143

of his age', to take into account everything that he took into account, and still to finish with an overwhelming affirmative vision.[9]

An admirable intention: but Wilson has been inclined to leave out a good deal of what Eliot and other 'pessimistic' writers of the twentieth century have taken account of.

Along with this repression of doubts goes a lack of respect for 'minute particulars'—those details, those objections, those tiny flaws, those irritating yet intractable little contradictions which break up our neat conceptual schemes, which plunge us into 'uncertainties, mysteries, doubts', and yet which force us to rethink, rebuild. Like H. G. Wells, Wilson could claim 'an inherent tendency to get things ruthlessly mapped out and consistent' which makes him neglect 'minute particulars'[10]; but it is out of 'minute particulars', as well as grand conceptions, that cathedrals are built.

All this means that Wilson's affirmative vision can lack substance; it seems to take off into the void. R. D. Laing has said: 'As long as the self remains "uncommitted to the objective element", it is free to dream or imagine anything.'[11] In his novels, Wilson can sometimes appear 'uncommitted to the objective element', although he would claim to be committed to a greater objectivity. The self soars up, generates a manic euphoria (one version of the 'peak experience'?), but the real world is untouched, unchanged. This lack of commitment to the objective element is most evident in the science fiction novels, especially the first two of them, and accounts for their air of arbitrary fantasy. Wilson, living in a world where 'things do not happen', seeks reality, but he does so in the mind, not in the outside world: the world of detail, of minute particulars, of contradiction, of negativity, of uncertainties, mysteries, doubts, suffering: the world which subverts dogmatic optimism. He seeks escape from the prison of the mind within the mind. There, he will escape solipsism; there, he will find reality. But he may only flee further into himself, further away from reality. In this void, only God gives reality; but Wilson rejects God. Thus he remains suspended between two realities; he denies the reality of God, but rejects the access to reality which the physical world, other people, human society can provide.

It is not surprising that he has to invoke the Life Force and similar substitutes for the Deity.

Obviously Wilson's tendency to withdraw from everyday reality has been increased by his seclusion in Cornwall. To some extent, this was a necessary survival measure after the critical reaction against him in the late 1950s; but it was also a response to profound personal promptings. Of course, Wilson is not a hermit, but a married man with children and many friends; he frequently travels in England and abroad, writes many reviews and articles, and appears from time to time on radio and television; but he remains dedicated to the 'life of the mind' rather than the shared human world. He would argue that this is necessary to create the body of work that he hopes will ultimately contribute to the evolutionary advance of mankind; but he himself recognizes that 'there is a danger in being just a thinker: being an intellectual is a kind of suicide, living outside the vitality of life'.[12] It is particularly dangerous for a novelist, because novelists are energized by the 'vitality of life', and much of that is to be found in the shared human world. But withdrawal is in Wilson's blood; he has said that he has no doubt that if, in his teens, 'some good fairy had made me a present of a life annuity I would have found my "tower" and produced the kind of works suited to a pessimist and a recluse—some kind of combination of Schopenhauer, Firbank, and Lovecraft.'[13] In adult life he has found, if not a tower, a cottage in Cornwall; and his later novels, at least, could be seen as those of an optimist and a recluse.

If Wilson's novels are turned away from life in some respects, however, in other ways they go forward to meet it. This is where their strengths lie. Wilson's use of popular forms is an interesting attempt to bridge the gap between serious and popular literature which exists perhaps more than ever before in our own century. As Robert Scholes says:

> the vacuum left by the movement of 'serious' fiction away from storytelling has been filled by popular forms with few pretentions to any virtues beyond those of narrative excitement. But the very emptiness of these forms, as they are usually managed, has left another gap, for forms which supply readers' needs for narration without starving their needs for intellection.[14]

145

Wilson's use of popular forms aims to supply readers' needs for narration without starving their needs for intellection. Of course, he is not the only present-day novelist to use these forms in such a way; and we have seen that he sometimes exemplifies the danger of the technique, which is that the writer may fall to the level of the form he sets out to elevate. But the novelist today has a choice: either esotericism, which is increasingly likely to mean non-publication, and that, if prolonged too long, may mean creative death; or the attempt to reach a wider audience by making use of some aspects of mass culture. In the visual arts in the 1960s, the Pop Art movement tried to reorient the attitude of the modern artist to mass culture; instead of remaining aloof from it, he should welcome it, enter into it, employ its energies and communicative powers. Wilson has tried to do this in the novel. As with Pop Art, the result has sometimes been debasing; at other times, it has pointed out a new road for the writer. Brought up himself on mass culture—comics, films, *True Detective* magazines, gangster thrillers, science fiction—Wilson knows its power to stimulate the imagination and to stand for deeper concerns; a debased, abused power, but a power nonetheless, which is fuelled from a deep, ancient source. For popular forms are debased myths: carriers of the mythopoeic power which once bound together and explained the universe. The old myths are broken, but the mythic impulse remains strong, and it is mass culture which now does most of the work of trying to satisfy it. Of course, it is too superficial to satisfy it properly; but it retains the elements which could be used to create more satisfying myths. In his unashamed use of popular forms for purportedly serious ends, Wilson is still viewed with some suspicion by his age; but it may well be that, in a good sense, he anticipates the future.

It may also be that he anticipates the future by setting out, against the *Zeitgeist*, to try and map it positively. Dennis Donoghue points out:

> Society . . . has received the artist's message that we are all sick, alienated, and so forth. The deepest visions of alienation are now blurred for general consumption and sold at cut-price. This mode of criticism is no longer available. . . . The artist who would criticize our society at this moment would probably

hold up before its eyes a heroic image, the implication being that we are incapable of rising to it. There is a literature of celebration as well as a literature of critique.[15]

Pessimism has become modish, and it is, as Wilson constantly reiterates, sometimes the easier option. 'Facing up to the harsh reality of life' provides an excuse, a noble justification, for inaction. Nothing to be done. Wilson's novels, his whole *oeuvre*, are an attempt, a virtually one-man attempt in contemporary culture, to hold up a heroic image of man, to produce a literature of celebration. If it does not altogether succeed, this is partly because our language of heroism and celebration has worn thin. It seems archaic and false. The dominant linguistic modes are pessimistic, carriers of defeat and despair. Wilson, however, believes that the writer must be prepared to work alone, unsupported by his age, fighting against its language, creating his own concepts, his own language, in the hope that they may one day become common concepts, a common language, the Everlasting Gospel of evolutionary man. To reaffirm the point made in Chapter Two: Wilson is attempting to create a re-definition of man in the light of the future. Of the positive future.

This is the greatest value of his novels. We live at what is perhaps the most decisive point in human history. There is the apocalyptic prospect: nuclear destruction on a worldwide scale, then the rebuilding of civilization from the beginning, in a devastated ecosphere. But suppose this does not happen? Suppose the nuclear threat is held off, and we move forward, into the twenty-first century, into the twenty-second. The year 2000, once the symbol of tomorrow for science fiction writers and futurologists, is only eighteen years away now; it is a truism that change is happening more quickly than ever before, especially in the sciences. We must prepare for the future, in spite of the possibility of nuclear destruction, as we prepare for our own futures, although we may die tomorrow. The novel can help us to do that—to re-define ourselves in the light of the future. In doing that, the novel may also make a future for itself.

Wilson has recognized and helped to define this function of the novel. It is not only in his science fiction that he looks forward: all his fiction looks to the future. It makes the 'thought-

147

experiment' of assuming that man does have a positive future, and attempts to work out the implications of that, not only for the future, but also for man as he is at present. In this sense, all his novels are science fiction—or future fiction. We may, of course, disagree with the re-definition of man that Wilson proposes; but, in a sense, that does not matter. As Shaw said in his 'Postscript' to *Back to Methuselah*:

> Both [philosophers and scientists] are trying to see a little further in the dark; and whether the electronic microscope or the philosopher's brain has pierced it farthest is not worth quarrelling about; for the darkness beyond still forces us to tolerate both microscopic revelation and metaphysical speculation with all its guesses and hypotheses and dramatizations of how far thought can reach.[16]

In his novels, Wilson gives us hypotheses and dramatizations of how far thought can reach; and in future fictions, as in scientific hypotheses, it can sometimes be more important to be stimulating than to be right. Wilson's fictions express his manifesto for the future clearly and squarely; they do not compromise or hedge bets; and thus they provoke us to challenge, to argue, to think for ourselves about the nature of man, a nature which no longer seems fixed and immutable, and which is defined, not only by the past, but also, more than ever, by the future. The twenty-first century may look back on Colin Wilson as one of the novelists who foresaw the future of fiction, and something, perhaps, of the future of man.

NOTES

1. In a letter to this author.
2. *The Schoolgirl Murder Case* (Hart Davis, MacGibbon, 1974; my refs. to Panther, 1975 ed.), p. 204.
3. 'Note', *God of the Labyrinth*, p. 276.
4. A copy of the typescript of *The Magician from Siberia*, and details of the *Lulu* novel, were supplied by Mr. Wilson to this author, and the discussion is based on these.
5. *Angry Decade*, p. 160.
6. Cf. F. R. Leavis: '[Arnold] Bennett seems . . . never to have been disturbed enough by life to come anywhere near greatness.' *The Great Tradition* (Chatto & Windus, 1948, my ref. to Pelican, 1972 ed.), p. 16.

7. Keats's letter to G. and T. Keats, 13 January 1818.
8. Nigel Dennis, 'Emphasize the Positive', *Sunday Telegraph* (14 May 1972), p. 16.
9. *World of Colin Wilson*, p. 186.
10. *Expt in Autobiography*, II, p. 620.
11. R. D. Laing, *The Divided Self* (Tavistock, 1960; my ref. to Pelican, 1965 ed.), p. 89.
12. Interview with Timothy Wilson. See Chapter Five, n. 23 above.
13. *Voyage*, p. 42.
14. *Structural Fabulation*, p. 40.
15. Dennis Donoghue, 'Dangling Man' in *The Ordinary Universe* (Faber, 1968), p. 217.
16. 'Postscript' (1944), *Back to Methuselah*, pp. 317–18.

Bibliography

Original publishers and dates of the English editions are given. Where later editions have been used in this study, details are given in the Notes and References for each chapter.

1 Novels by Colin Wilson

This lists all Wilson's novels to date.

Ritual in the Dark (Gollancz, 1960)
Adrift in Soho (Gollancz, 1961)
The World of Violence (Gollancz, 1963)
Man Without A Shadow (Barker, 1963)
Necessary Doubt (Barker, 1964)
The Glass Cage (Barker, 1966)
The Mind Parasites (Barker, 1967)
The Philosopher's Stone (Barker, 1969)
The Killer (New English Library, 1970)
The God of the Labyrinth (Hart Davis, 1970)
The Black Room (Weidenfeld & Nicolson, 1971)
The Schoolgirl Murder Case (Hart Davis, MacGibbon, 1974)
The Space Vampires (Hart Davis, MacGibbon, 1976)

Wilson has also written a novella, *The Return of the Lloigor* (Village Press, 1974). This was originally published in an anthology of tales based on H. P. Lovecraft's private mythology: *Tales of the Cthulhu Mythos* (Sauk City, U.S.A., Arkham House, 1969).

2 Non-fiction by Colin Wilson

The books most relevant to this study are listed here.

(a) Autobiography

Voyage to a Beginning (Woolf, 1969)
See also 'An Autobiographical Introduction' to *Religion and the Rebel* (details below).

(b) General Ideas

The Outsider (Gollancz, 1956)
Religion and the Rebel (Gollancz, 1957)
Beyond the Outsider: The Philosophy of the Future (Barker, 1965)
Introduction to the New Existentialism (Hutchinson, 1966)

(c) Psychology

New Pathways in Psychology: Maslow and the Post-Freudian Revolution (Gollancz, 1972)
Frankenstein's Castle: The Double Brain: Door to Wisdom (Ashgrove Press, 1980)

(d) Sexuality

Origins of the Sexual Impulse (Barker, 1963)

(e) Murder

A Casebook of Murder (Frewin, 1969)
Order of Assassins: The Psychology of Murder (Hart Davis, 1972)

(f) The Occult

The Occult (Hodder & Stoughton, 1971)
Mysteries: An Investigation into the Occult, the Paranormal and the Supernatural (Hodder & Stoughton, 1978)

(g) Literature

The Age of Defeat (Gollancz, 1959)
The Strength to Dream: Literature and the Imagination (Gollancz, 1962)
Eagle and Earwig (John Baker, 1965)
Bernard Shaw: A Reassessment (Hutchinson, 1969)
Poetry and Mysticism (Hutchinson, 1970)
Hesse, Reich, Borges (Village Press, 1974)
The Craft of the Novel (Gollancz, 1975)

151

3 Studies of Wilson

These either deal wholly with Wilson, or make substantial reference to him.

Allsop, Kenneth, *The Angry Decade* (Peter Owen, 1958)

Campion, Sidney R., *The World of Colin Wilson* (Muller, 1962)

Dillard, Richard H. W., 'Towards an Existential Realism: The Novels of Colin Wilson', *Hollins Critic*, vol. iv, no. 4 (October, 1967, Hollins College, Virginia, U.S.A.)

Holroyd, Stuart, *Contraries: A Personal Progression* (Bodley Head, 1975)

Weigel, John A., *Colin Wilson* (Boston, Twayne's English Authors Series no. 181, 1975)

Index

Novels and non-fiction by Colin Wilson are indexed under title.